❧

The School of Mary

Other books
from Sophia Institute Press®
by John A. Kane:

*Conquering Your Sins
With Heartfelt Repentance*

*Transforming Your Life
Through the Eucharist*

John A. Kane

The School of Mary

Forty Essential Lessons for Sinners,
from the Blessed Mother Herself

SOPHIA INSTITUTE PRESS®
Manchester, New Hampshire

The School of Mary: Forty Essential Lessons for Sinners, from the Blessed Mother Herself was originally published without a subtitle in 1942 by St. Anthony Guild Press, Paterson, New Jersey. This 1999 edition by Sophia Institute Press contains minor editorial revisions to the original text.

Jacket design by Lorraine Bilodeau

The cover artwork is a detail of Gerard David's *La Vierge à la soupe au lait Maria met de paplepel*, Musées royaux des Beaux-Arts de Belgique, Bruxelles–Koninklijke Musea voor Schone Kunsten van België, Brussel (photo courtesy of Speltdoorn).

Sophia Institute Press®
Box 5284, Manchester, NH 03108
1-800-888-9344
www.sophiainstitute.com

Nihil obstat: Henry J. Zolzer, Censor
Imprimatur: Thomas H. McLaughlin, Bishop of Paterson
May 1, 1942

Library of Congress Cataloging-in-Publication Data

Kane, John A., 1883-
 The school of Mary : forty essential lessons for sinners, from the Blessed Mother herself / John A. Kane.
  p. cm.
 Originally published: Paterson, N.J. : St. Anthony Guild Press, 1942.
 ISBN 0-918477-98-0 (pbk. : alk. paper)
 1. Mary, Blessed Virgin, Saint Biography. 2. Christian saints —
Palestine Biography. 3. Christian life — Catholic authors. I. Title.
BT605.2.K26   1999
232.91 — dc21   99-15072 CIP

99 00 01 02 03 10 9 8 7 6 5 4 3 2 1

*To the gracious memory
of my father and mother, who
first taught me by precept and example
devotion to her who is our life,
our sweetness, and our hope*

Editor's note: The biblical references in the following pages are based on the Douay-Rheims edition of the Old and New Testaments. Where applicable, quotations have been cross-referenced with the differing names and numeration in the Revised Standard Version, using the following symbol: (RSV =).

Contents

∞

Foreword

The claim of our Blessed Lady to an essential place in
the universal religion is unquestionable, inalienable.
The consciousness of that fact was curiously manifested
when, in 1865, Catholic missionaries entered Nagasaki,
Japan, where no priest had been for more than two hun-
dred years. A little group of hereditary Christians who
lived there asked three questions of the newcomers, to
determine whether or not they were really priests of that
same ancient Faith which the edict of the shogun had
suppressed in 1614: Did they obey the Bishop of Rome?
Did they observe celibacy? Did they venerate the Mother
of God? The sure instinct of Catholic faith thus hit upon
the three central points of dogma, Catholic discipline,
and Catholic devotion.

It would be dishonest for Catholics to deny the superficial differences in the sentiments with which Christians

of all ages have exercised the right to look upon Mary, the Mother of Jesus, as their mother also. Likewise, it would be unpardonable for Protestants to ignore the substantial identity of those sentiments. In so exercising that right, they are but claiming the legacy bequeathed to them on Calvary, when St. John stood there — a sort of Adam — as our representative and heard the words "Behold thy mother." To be sure, from race to race, from age to age, from man to man, Catholic devotion does make its way along an amazing variety of approaches, but it remains ever the same in essential faith and love and loyalty. The shining of the same light is reflected in the all but tacit assumptions of the Gospel, in the rich rhetoric of the early Fathers, in the prose and poetry of Asiatic and European, Greek and Latin, Italian and Celt and Saxon.

Here in this book, another voice is lifted up. The author has joined that long procession which includes Ephraim and Chrysostom, Ambrose, Augustine and Jerome, Bernard and Thomas, Alphonsus and Newman and Faber and Claudel. Again we hear that sonorous, never-ending chant which marvelously — like the apostolic sermon on the first Pentecost — is understood by every people and tribe and nation and tongue.[1] Here, in America in our day, the soul of a priest is focused in meditation on the Mother of Jesus — her relationship to God, her relationship to us. And the result of his thinking, offered in this book, is simple and reverent enough to be fittingly offered to her whom all generations call blessed. It is solid and balanced and luminous enough to support, reassure, and enlighten thousands of her children.

Joseph McSorley, C.S.P.

---

[1] Acts 2:4-11.

❦

The School of Mary

Chapter One

∾

Commend yourself to Mary's care

The end of all devotion is Christ. "I am Alpha and Omega, the beginning and the end."[2] Christ is the cornerstone of our salvation, for "this is eternal life, that they may know Thee, the only true God, and Jesus Christ, whom Thou hast sent."[3] "There is no other name under Heaven given to men, whereby we must be saved."[4]

If Christ is not the rock upon which rests the spiritual edifice of our sanctification, then the edifice is doomed, and great will be the fall thereof. But if the edifice is founded upon Christ, then the winds of the tempter may blow and the rains of his temptations may fall and the floods of passion may rise and beat upon that

---

[2] Apoc. 1:8 (RSV = Rev. 1:8).

[3] John 17:3.

[4] Acts 4:12.

house, and it will not fall, because it is founded upon a rock.[5]

We must be one with Christ according to His words: "Abide in me, and I in you. As the branch cannot bear fruit of itself, unless it abide in the vine, so neither can you, unless you abide in me. I am the vine, you the branches. He that abideth in me, and I in him, the same beareth much fruit; for without me you can do nothing. If anyone abide not in me, he shall be cast forth as a branch and shall wither; and they shall gather him up and cast him into the fire, and he burneth."[6] We must be one with Christ because, Christ being our Mediator with His eternal Father, it is only "by Him and in Him and through Him that we can render all honor and glory" to the Father in the unity of the Holy Spirit. It is only through Christ that we can be holy ourselves and radiate holiness around us.

Now, devotion to Mary is devotion to Christ, because Mary has given us Christ. The humble Virgin was chosen by the eternal Father to shed upon a sinful world, without

[5] Cf. Luke 6:47-49.
[6] John 15:4-6.

lesion to her glorious virginity, its eternal light: Jesus
Christ, our Lord, the Savior of men.

But union with God was essential in order for Mary to
accomplish this, the most wondrous work ever given to a
mortal to perform. And Mary was most intimately united
with God, for the angelic ambassador said to her, "Hail,
full of grace, the Lord is with thee: blessed art thou among
women."[7] Mary's union with God has been most tersely
and accurately expressed by a child of genius. "Mary's
fullness of grace," says St. Thomas Aquinas, "was so great
that it brought her to a most intimate union with the
Author of grace; that this fitted her to receive into her
holy womb the One who contained all graces; and that
thus, in conceiving Him, she became, in some sort, the
source of that grace which He was to pour forth over all
mankind, and so concurred in giving the human race its
Deliverer."[8]

Mary's intimate union with her divine Son is the reason for her power with Him. "He that shall find me shall

---

[7] Luke 1:28.

[8] Cf. St. Thomas Aquinas (c. 1225-1274; Dominican
philosopher and theologian), *Summa Theologica*, III,
Q. 27, art. 5.

find life, and shall have salvation from the Lord."[9] "For God," says St. Bernard,[10] "who has given us His Son through Mary, has willed that we should obtain the graces He has merited for us by the intercession of Mary."

God, all-powerful though He is, could not bestow upon a creature a degree of honor higher than that conferred on His mother. He could not make her divine by nature, but He has, through the grace that He so freely lavished on her in virtue of the divine maternity, made her inseparable from Him in the salvation of souls. The heart of Christ and the heart of Mary beat in unison. When we love and honor the mother, we must necessarily love and honor the Son. The closer the union with Mary, the more intimate the association with Christ. He who will not have Mary for his mother, cannot have Christ for his Brother. The indissoluble union of Jesus and Mary established by the eternal Father and the Holy Spirit is the best proof of Mary's love for Christ and, consequently, for souls redeemed by the blood of Christ. Mary loves Christ because she is His mother, and she loves us because she is

[9] Prov. 8:35.
[10] St. Bernard (1090-1153), Abbot of Clairvaux.

our mother. From the revelations of our Lord to St. Gertrude,[11] Christ is Mary's firstborn according to the flesh, and we are her second-born according to the spirit. Through the oblation of her divine Son on Calvary, Mary, with a sorrow "great as the sea,"[12] brought us forth to a life of grace and thus became our spiritual mother.

Mary, our spiritual mother, heard the dying legacy of Jesus Christ: "Woman, behold thy son." After that, He said to the disciple John, "Behold thy mother."[13]

In His death agony, the infinite Lover of immortal souls ratified on Calvary the oblation that Mary makes for them, by giving them His mother to be their mother; for since all Christians form one body with Christ and are morally one person with Christ, St. John represented them on the mount of crucifixion.

Thou art, then, O Mary, after thy divine Son,
God's most precious gift to man.
Thy love for us, therefore, is inferior only to the love
of Him who purchased us at the cost of His life.

---

[11] St. Gertrude (1256-c. 1302), German mystic.
[12] Lam. 2:13.
[13] John 19:26-27.

Mary's love for us is the sum and soul of her powerful intercession for us with Christ. Hence, absolute trust in Mary's help is a necessary part of the virtue of hope. "I am the mother of fair love, and of fear, and of knowledge, and of holy hope. In me is all grace of the way and of the truth; in me is all hope of life and of virtue."[14] The hope of grace from God, the source of grace, however, will yield fruit and redound to our spiritual welfare only through our free cooperation. And the true Christian does all he can so that grace may benefit him.

But how high is the standard, how lofty the ideal, that is set for the true Christian! Never does human nature, with its myriad frailties, measure up to the standard; never does it realize the ideal. Impelled by the law of his own impotence, man can only soar upward on the wings of constant endeavor. Unaided, he can accomplish little; he is a social being, and since he lives, moves, and fulfills his destiny only in society, he is therefore dependent upon his neighbor. In the natural order, then, mutual assistance is a necessary consequence of man's mutual dependence, and in the supernatural order, it accords perfectly with

[14] Ecclus. 24:24-25.

Christian hope for one member of Christ's Mystical Body, the Church, to intercede for another.

The unbeliever sits in defiant judgment upon this truth and boldly proclaims, with all the assertiveness of error, that Catholics offer the Virgin Mother of God and the other saints divine worship. If praying to Mary and the other saints is identical with divine worship, the unbeliever must, by the force of his own false premises, arrive at a decidedly erroneous conclusion. The acceptance of such premises would fill the world with idolaters: when I solicit the aid of my neighbor, or when I beg his intercession for me, I am an idolater in the strict sense of the term.

This false reasoning ramifies in many directions, making devastating inroads upon man's nature as a social being and upon the domain of faith; for to state that men do not intercede for one another is to deny a very obvious fact of experience — to proclaim that man is not a social being. Such reasoning is, moreover, rebellion against Christ, the infallible Truth, who with His own lips taught us this mutual intercession. Such reasoning falsifies not only the Our Father, but also the admonition of the apostle: "Pray one for another, that you may be saved";[15] and therefore it is destructive of the unity of Christ's divine organism, since it divorces the Church Militant from the Church Triumphant in Heaven and the Church Suffering in Purgatory.[16] It is wrong to suppose that our brethren who have fallen asleep in the Lord do not intercede for us so that we, too, may obtain the incorruptible crown, because the beatitude of the saints consists in the possession of God, and therefore in loving all that God loves.

How consoling, how comforting, is this doctrine taught by the infallibly constituted exponent of truth, the Church — this doctrine that links earth with Heaven! It is inspiring to know that we have Christ, our elder Brother, "always living to make intercession for us"[17] and the saints whose names we bear, and Mary, the Queen of Saints, ever pleading for us before the throne of mercy in God's eternal kingdom. And oh, the power of

---

[15] James 5:16.

[16] The Church Militant comprises all the members of the Church on earth, the Church Triumphant, the members in Heaven, and the Church Suffering, the souls in Purgatory.

[17] Heb. 7:25.

Mary's intercession — Mary, loved by the Father as the mother of His Son, loved by the Son as His own mother, and loved by the Holy Spirit as His most pure spouse! "He that shall find me shall find life, and shall have salvation from the Lord."

Human eloquence, poetry, and art all fail to describe Mary's power, the true genesis of which is her great love for us. That love we can never question when we consider the sacrifices that she made, in union with her divine Son, for our salvation. In our redemption, according to the eternal plans of an all-merciful God, Mary was morally indispensable. Fatal, then, is the delusion that we can progress spiritually without the help of our mother.

In the natural order, there is something abnormal in the physical development of a child who loses his mother in his earliest and tenderest years. The same truth holds in the supernatural order. Without our spiritual mother's unfailing love and fostering care from our very birth, progress in virtue is impossible. But to establish our claim to Mary's help, we must imitate her virtues, especially her humility, her purity, and her love of God.

The practice of these virtues will shelter us under the protecting folds of her maternal mantle. With Mary's aid, we will be ever on our guard against the treacherous cunning of all the enemies of our soul. We will meet their full assaults with intrepid determination and their hostile charges with fearless courage. We will be devoted to the service of God.

> *To thy protection, then, Virgin Most Powerful,*
> *we thy children commend ourselves with a confidence*
> *born of thy great love for those who, like thee,*
> *are humble and pure, and love God above all things.*
> *In the stern struggle for salvation, the mightiest*
> *and most momentous of all struggles, help us.*
> *Forsake us not until our enemies are conquered*
> *and the spoils of victory are ours forever!*

Chapter Two

∞

Learn to use the grace
God gives you

It is an article of Faith that the Blessed Virgin, eternally predestined to be the Mother of Christ, was from the first instant of her conception preserved free from the guilt of Original Sin. This singular privilege is called her Immaculate Conception.

"It was meet," says St. Irenaeus,[18] "that the God of all purity should spring from the greatest purity, from the most pure bosom." "Such a privilege," St. Anselm[19] tells us, "was suitable to her dignity. It was possible for God to confer it; hence He conferred it." So also does Origen[20] say, "She was not contaminated by the breath of the

---

[18] St. Irenaeus (c. 130-c. 200), Bishop of Lyons.
[19] St. Anselm (c. 1033-1109), Archbishop of Canterbury.
[20] Origen (c. 185-c. 254), Alexandrian biblical critic, exegete, theologian, and spiritual writer.

serpent." And finally, St. John Damascene[21] declares, "To her the serpent had no access."

Alone of all the children of Adam, Mary was gifted with the fullness of sanctifying grace, which made her the object of a distinct, transcendent love on the part of the Most High. We may indeed imagine the beatified hosts exclaiming, upon beholding her incomparable holiness, "Who is she that cometh forth as the morning rising, fair as the moon, bright as the sun, terrible as an army set in array?"[22] She had the use of reason, and began to advance to the most sublime perfection, from the very moment her body and soul were united. Immeasurably beyond the power of the human mind to conceive — much less understand — are the workings of divine Omnipotence to render Mary a fitting habitation for the Redeemer of the world.

With no tendency to evil — with, on the contrary, a most marked propensity to the highest virtue — she glorified God more than all His other creatures did. Never did she yield to the least imperfection, let alone sin. At

---

[21] St. John Damascene (c. 675-c. 749), Greek theologian.

[22] Cant. 6:9 (RSV = Song of Sol. 6:9).

the very instant of her conception, her intellect was illumined with the light of God, and her will was wholly conformed to the divine will. She was without ignorance and concupiscence, the fountainheads from which flow the sin and suffering of men. Ever subjecting them to the commands of reason and the influence of grace, she maintained her empire over her mind and heart, regulating her thoughts, desires, and deeds by the wondrous actual graces of which she was the loving recipient. She had no conflict with vice from within or from without. Her extreme hatred and horror of sin was the measure of her supreme love of virtue. Singular purity of intention, by which she surrendered herself entirely to God in the minutest details of her life, and absolute forgetfulness of herself, by which she was most intimately united with God — that was the impregnable foundation of Mary's sanctity.

Is it possible to imitate such sanctity? We must imitate Christ, the God of infinite sanctity, who became man not only to redeem us, but also to propose Himself as a model for our imitation. The fact that we are frail mortals does not excuse us from failing to copy His example. Now, if the Gospel enjoins upon us the imitation of Christ, we can by no means dispense ourselves from striving after the perfection of Mary.

But our imitation of both Jesus and Mary depends upon and is measured by our response to the amount of grace that God sees fit to give us. We must always bear in mind that the holiness of the Blessed Virgin was not the result of the marvelous gratuitous privilege of her Immaculate Conception nor of the inestimable degree of sanctifying grace that God had conferred on her. Mary's surpassing sanctity flowed from the permanent dedication of herself to God at the moment of reason and her constant corre-spondence with actual grace thereafter.

We, too, can, however imperfectly, consecrate our-selves irrevocably to the service of God by steadfast fidel-ity to the degree of grace that He condescends to bestow upon us. And should we have the misfortune of revoking this, our free oblation of ourselves to our Lord and Master, we can — for God is love — regain by contrition what we have lost by sin. God demands of us only a reason-able service. He does not reap where He has not sown. He asks us only to be generous with Him by turning to good account the graces that He ever lavishes on us, by humbling ourselves at the sight of our myriad sins and multiple imperfections, and by rising promptly when we fall, with renewed confidence in His mercy.

Every being acts according to his nature. God, because He is perfect, could propose only perfect models for our imitation. But although perfect, they are nevertheless suitable for our imitation. Were not grace always at our disposal, we should be able to accuse God of injustice for asking us to do what human nature without divine help could never accomplish. But aided from on high, especially by Mary, who, of all the saints (since she is their queen), has the most influence with her divine Son, we shall, as true children of our heavenly mother, grow daily into her likeness.

Pray for us,
O holy Mother of God and our mother,
that we may imitate thy virtues,
and so may be made worthy of
the promises of Christ.

Chapter Three

∞

Love God above all else

On November 21, the Church celebrates the feast of the Presentation of the Blessed Virgin in the Temple. This feast is entirely different from the feast of the Presentation of Christ in the Temple, when Mary submitted to the law of the purification.[23]

From her earliest days, the Mother of God dedicated herself to His love and service. She was led by divine inspiration to His house; her dispositions corresponded to the degree of grace that was hers and merited for her an increase of grace prolific of her marvelous progress in the science of the saints. In silence and solitude, and with her entire preoccupation with her God, which the ceremonies of the Temple greatly facilitated, she gradually prepared herself for her sublime dignity. Although the

[23] Cf. Lev. 12:2-8.

designs of God were unknown to her, she nevertheless attuned the ears of her soul to catch the faintest whisper of His voice, and strove, by deepening her appreciation of her own nothingness and by absolute and decisive detachment from the world, for the closest possible union with Him.

In silence and obscurity, the voice of God is most articulate. True piety shuns publicity. Obedient to Christ's command — "So let your light shine before men that they may see your good works and glorify your Father who is in Heaven"[24] — the deeply religious soul seeks to be known only when the glory of God is at stake. Great souls who live for God alone are usually silent and solitary even in the midst of the madding crowd's ignoble strife. They are in the world, but not of the world. Fully dedicated to the service of God, they are dead to the world and dead to themselves.

So we can picture Mary alone with her God, a stranger to all others, even to those who dwelt with her in the enclosure of the Temple. Angelically modest and absorbingly recollected, rapt in silent prayer with God, who was

[24] Matt. 5:16.

the be-all and the end-all of her life, and therefore utterly forgetful of herself, she made no show of her interior ineffable sanctity as she followed, without singularity and with rare devotion and exactitude, the life led in common by the virgins of God's house. Although deeply earnest about her duties and wholly intent on their performance, she gave her companions no occasion to divine the marvelous fullness of grace with which God had dowered her virginal soul. But although she concealed her unique and truly remarkable spiritual gifts, the odor of virtue that she diffused around her was all the more redolent.

Words are, however, impotent to describe the heavenly beauty that adorned her finely sensitive soul as she was being prepared by the eternal Father to be the mother of His divine Son and the spouse of His Holy Spirit. Wisdom was building itself a house;[25] the omnipotence of God was constructing a living temple for the Savior of mankind.

The soul of man has been formed and fashioned by God to be His temple. "You are the temple of the living

[25] Cf. Prov. 9:1.

God; as God saith: I will dwell in them."[26] Are we the temple of the living God? Not if our souls are enamored of "the earth and the fullness thereof."[27] If our souls enthrone an idol — be that idol pride, avarice, lust, or love of the good things of the world — far from being the temple of the living God, they are the sinful abode of the demons of Hell. "Love not the world, nor the things which are in the world. If any man love the world, the charity of the Father is not in him. For all that is in the world is the concupiscence of the flesh and the concupiscence of the eyes and the pride of life. . . . The world passeth away and the concupiscence thereof, but he that doth the will of God abideth forever."[28]

No matter what our calling, reason itself, not to mention revelation, dictates the undivided consecration of ourselves to the love and service of God. We cannot follow simultaneously principles that are mutually exclusive and hence essentially contradictory. What reason teaches, Christ enforces when He states very explicitly, "No man can serve two masters. For either he will hate the one

[26] 2 Cor. 6:16.
[27] Ps. 23:1 (RSV = Ps. 24:1).
[28] 1 John 2:15-17.

and love the other, or he will sustain the one and despise the other. You cannot serve God and mammon."[29] "Thou shalt love the Lord thy God with thy whole heart and with thy whole soul and with thy whole mind. This is the greatest and the first commandment."[30] "The Lord thy God shalt thou adore, and Him only shalt thou serve."[31]

The love of God above all things, inspired by the conscious recognition of His infinite greatness and our utter nothingness, and energized by our complete, unequivocal, permanent detachment from the world and its unsatisfactory pleasures, will make our souls, as it made the soul of Mary, the temple of the living God. "If anyone love me, he will keep my word. And my Father will love him, and we will come to him and will make our abode with him."[32] To be known to God and unknown to men, to possess God and to be forgotten by creatures — this, after the example of Mary, should be the consuming yearning of our souls. God will dwell in us, and we will

[29] Matt. 6:24.
[30] Matt. 22:37-38.
[31] Matt. 4:10.
[32] John 14:23.

live to Him alone only through persevering prayer and habitual recollection, which, making God the beginning and the end of our thoughts, words, and actions, will direct our entire lives to His greater honor and glory.

Chapter Four

Learn Mary's spirit of self-forgetfulness

How old the Blessed Mother was when she vowed her virginity to God, we do not know. We do know that her consecration was inspired by the Holy Spirit and was preceded by a perfect prevision of its consequences.

Marriage and motherhood were the cherished ideals of every Jewish maiden. Even the daughters of the tribe of Levi, dedicated to the service of the priests or indeed of the high priest, all married without exception, because Jewish women, with their intense love for maternity, reprobated sterility. Thus was Mary's vow truly unique, and it branded her with a kind of stigma, opposing as it did the honored traditions of the Jews.

As the Blessed Virgin was full of grace and thereby absolutely free from the sting of the flesh, her vow accorded completely with her natural desires, and consequently the sacrifices associated with it are in no way to be measured by the voluntary surrender of the joys of married life. Mary's body was on earth, but her soul was in Heaven. The Lord being her portion,[33] she renounced all else — honors, dignities, the pleasures and rewards of marriage — and joyously chose the life of a virgin; she chose, that is, to be entirely disengaged from the world, and hidden.

In order to appreciate Mary's oblation of herself by her vow of virginity, we must look higher. None knew better than she the meaning of the prophecy: "And thou, Bethlehem Ephrata, art a little one among the thousands of Juda: out of thee shall He come forth unto me that is to be the Ruler in Israel; and His going forth is from the beginning, from the days of eternity."[34] She understood that Christ was to be born at the time in which she lived and was to descend from David's family, which was her own.

Jews and Gentiles both were expecting the Messiah, but they had lost sight of the prophecy of Isaiah: "Behold, a virgin shall conceive and bear a Son, and His name

[33] Cf. Ps. 118:57 (RSV = Ps. 119:57).
[34] Mic. 5:2.

shall be called Emmanuel."[35] They had not grasped the truth that the birth of Christ was to be accompanied by a miracle that would never be repeated: a virgin would become a mother.

It would seem, then, that Mary, in consecrating her virginity to God, had given up all hope of becoming the mother of Christ, because her vow, being a free act, was made with the clear foreknowledge of its consequences. It was the product of her profound humility and of a deep, settled conviction that she was not worthy of the supreme honor of the divine maternity; and hence, a jealous thought of her who would be the favored recipient of so signal and surpassing a dignity could not even shadow, much less enter, her mind.

Such humility God will reward munificently. Mary's self-extinction prepared her for the reception of the unspeakable gift of the divine motherhood — actually made her the Mother of God: "He hath regarded the humility of His handmaid."[36] "Mary," says St. Bernard, "pleased God by her virginity, but she conceived Him by her humility."

---

[35] Isa. 7:14.
[36] Luke 1:48.

How unsearchable are the ways of God! He often chooses means that, humanly speaking, are inadequate to accomplish their ends. What a luminous illustration of this truth is the fact that He demanded, although the Jews lacked all sympathy with it, the state of virginity in her who was to be the mother of His divine Son, and made the renunciation of the divine maternity the price of its possession.

Like our mother Mary, we should never desire to be great before God or even before our fellowman. "Every proud man is an abomination to the Lord."[37] "He hath had regard to the prayer of the humble, and He hath not despised their petition."[38] "Nor from the beginning have the proud been acceptable to Thee, but the prayer of the humble and the meek hath always pleased Thee."[39]

God loves to build on nothing. "What hast thou that thou hast not received? And if thou hast received, why dost thou glory, as if thou hadst not received it?"[40]

[37] Prov. 16:5.
[38] Ps. 101:18 (RSV = Ps. 102:17).
[39] Jth. 9:16.
[40] 1 Cor. 4:7.

Learn Mary's spirit of self-forgetfulness

Once we realize our nothingness, and consequently our unprofitableness, God will work such miracles of grace within us as will raise the edifice of our sanctity to supreme heights. We should not anticipate the designs of God, but should wait patiently until He decides to use us as instruments to advance His interests on earth. Nor should we be surprised if He adopts means wholly repugnant to flesh and blood.

The greater glory of God through total forgetfulness of ourselves must be the aim of our lives. This is only keeping the greatest and first commandment of the Law, only giving to God what is His by divine right. Humility, then, is our sorest need. If we seek the glory of God in everything and entirely forego ourselves, we will travel the surest and the swiftest road to Heaven. Who, after Christ, was humbler than Mary? Yet who, after Christ, gave God greater glory? Far from contravening the designs of divine wisdom, Mary's humility only served to expedite the most eventful manifestation of God's infinite mercy to fallen man.

Chapter Five

~

Walk by the light of divine faith

Mary's vow of virginity was without precedent, and a
secret between her and her God. It is hardly likely that
her parents, if they were still alive, had the least inkling
of it, for the obvious reason that, conditioned by the
Jews' love of motherhood, they would indubitably have
opposed it.

To conceal the miraculous conception and birth of
His divine Son, the eternal Father inspired Joseph, who,
like Mary, was of the tribe of Juda and the family of David,
to marry this specially favored child of Heaven. Her parents consented, and Mary and Joseph were not only be-
trothed but probably married before the Annunciation by
the archangel Gabriel.

Before entering upon her new state of life, the Blessed
Virgin was forced to reveal to Joseph her consecration to
God, and to ask him to respect it. Being a just man, and

thus given to the practice of virtue in its most comprehensive sense, Joseph espoused Mary and lived with her a life of spotless virginity.

In this critical circumstance of her life, in order that she might be without misgiving as to the keeping of her vow, and might at the same time manifest to Joseph an attitude that was gracious, cordial, and symbolic of the marital relationship, the Blessed Mother did not trust to the fidelity of a mortal, but abandoned herself to Divine Providence. Her love of the virtue that makes man like an angel was the measure of her abandonment. With absolute confidence in the protection of God — for "he that dwelleth in the aid of the Most High shall abide under the protection of the God of Heaven"[41] — and absorbed by the concentrated contemplation of Him, she implicitly entrusted herself to her chaste spouse as to God Himself, supremely confident that the Holy Spirit, who had inspired the consecration of her virginity to God, would, with the invigorating power of His grace, enable her to preserve her purity in all its brilliant splendor.

[41] Ps. 90:1 (RSV = Ps. 91:1).

∞

What an example for us! Like Mary, we must never question the will of God, no matter how trying the test, but must make that will the pivot of our lives. How slow we are to realize that nothing happens except through God's ordination or permission. Knowing what is best for us, since He is infinitely wise, and loving us with an everlasting love, He ever takes into account our dearest interests.

A life of strong, living faith is a life of unwavering submission to Divine Providence. Convinced of this truth, we will never permit the dictates of human prudence to enter into the equation of our conformity to the divine will. The inspiration of grace, confirmed by lawful authority, will be our only guide.

Had Mary yielded to self-will, she would not have espoused Joseph. Had she listened to fallible reason, she would have necessarily concluded that such a union would mean the breaking of her vow, and so she would have rebelled against the divine will. With the future shrouded in mystery, and being herself utterly unable to forecast the outcome of her espousal with Joseph, powerless even to fancy by what conjuncture of circumstances

God would accomplish His will in her regard, she stifled all thought of herself, sacrificed reason to faith, and commended herself with childlike trust to Him who "reacheth from end to end mightily and ordereth all things sweetly."[42]

In doing the will of God, which is for us the goal of life, we must, after the example of our mother Mary, be enlightened, not by human wisdom, but by divine faith. The supernatural life of the soul, created by Baptism, is as real as the natural life of the body. This truth, which we are very prone to forget, St. Paul emphasizes when he writes to the Romans: "We are debtors, not to the flesh, to live according to the flesh. For if you live according to the flesh, you shall die, but if, by the Spirit, you mortify the deeds of the flesh, you shall live. For whosoever are led by the Spirit of God, they are the sons of God."[43] Again, he says, "They that are Christ's have crucified their flesh, with the vices and concupiscences."[44]

Unlike the light of weak, finite reason, which of itself cannot further our progress in virtue, the light of divine

[42] Wisd. 8:1.
[43] Rom. 8:12-14.
[44] Gal. 5:24.

faith, if we live in its reflected splendor, will enable us to conquer the cravings of the flesh and to escape life's pit-falls. It will conduct us safely to the God who has made us for Himself.

Chapter Six

∽

Do not hunger for special graces

Within a humble home in an obscure corner of the
earth — Nazareth in Galilee, the poorest and most
insignificant part of Judea — the Holy Spirit will perform
a miracle that will be the masterpiece of infinite power:
the Incarnation of the Son of God. It is by one of His
glorious archangels that God sends this most momentous
message ever delivered to man, announcing the advent of
the Savior of the world and the selection of the Virgin
Mary, the humblest of all creatures, to be His mother.
Thus is fulfilled the promise that Christ will be born of
the family of David, but not until that family is impoverished and has sunk into utter insignificance. A poor arti-
san is chosen to be the spouse of Mary and the foster
father of the Redeemer of men.

How striking the contrast between the circumstances
surrounding the birth of the Messiah and the glowing

pictures heralding the glory of His reign! Isaiah had prophesied, "A Child is born to us, and a Son is given to us, and the government is upon His shoulder; and His name shall be called Wonderful, Counselor, God the Mighty, the Father of the world to come, the Prince of Peace. His empire shall be multiplied, and there shall be no end of peace. He shall sit upon the throne of David and upon his kingdom, to establish it and strengthen it with judgment and with justice, from henceforth and forever."[45] "Rejoice and praise, O thou habitation of Sion, for great is He that is in the midst of thee, the Holy One of Israel."[46] The glory and the grandeur, the might and the magnificence of His reign shall spring, not from earth, but from Heaven, for His kingdom will not be of this world. The contempt of men will show His greatness before God. His parents must be unhonored and unknown, and their humility must be even greater than their poverty.

Inspired by the Holy Spirit and therefore with heavenly homage, the angelic ambassador salutes Mary with

[45] Isa. 9:6-7.
[46] Isa. 12:6.

the divinely eloquent words: "Hail, full of grace, the Lord is with thee. Blessed art thou among women."[47] Never before this did angel greet man with the word *hail*, but unlike the rest of mortals, Mary has a pre-eminent humility that is immune to the least suggestion of pride arising from such a salutation. She is declared by the mouthpiece of God to be "full of grace." But she is far from puffed up by this unheard-of praise; on the contrary, her humility sinks to immeasurable depths, for, while admitting the truth of the words, she attributes it to God alone working wondrously within her.

"The Lord is with thee," continues the heavenly herald. Yes, He is with her by His grace, and soon He will be with her by His corporeal presence, for He will be bone of her bones, and flesh of her flesh.[48]

Under the inspiration of the Holy Spirit, Gabriel waxes still more eloquent: "Blessed art thou among women." Mary's blessedness is due to her supreme sanctity. She will be hailed by all generations as blessed above all other women because she is the Mother of God and at the

---

[47] Luke 1:28.
[48] Cf. Gen. 2:23.

same time a spotless virgin. With the most precious gift of Heaven, God will reward the love of virginity that urges her not to accept the proffered dignity.

Her humility was so profound that Mary could hardly believe the commendation of the angelic envoy. And oh, how pleasing was her humility to God! He read her heart. He saw that she would not yield to the subtle and very strong temptation to pride flowing from the bestowal of His praise by His delegated messenger. The more her humility was tried, the more lowly she became in her own estimation.

Never must we yearn for the special graces given to the saints as a reward for their virtue. We should never aspire to nor anticipate them, but, like the Blessed Mother, we should render ourselves as worthy of them as possible by a humility that will make us realize that, as far as God is concerned, when we have done all things well, we are only unprofitable servants.[49]

It is the most cogent proof of our overweening pride to think that God gives us His best gifts just because we

---

[49] Cf. Luke 17:10.

hanker after them. Humility is the price of God's most precious favors. "Every proud man is an abomination to the Lord."[50] "God resisteth the proud and giveth grace to the humble."[51] "The Lord will destroy the house of the proud."[52] "God hath overturned the thrones of proud princes, and hath set up the meek in their stead."[53] "Before destruction, the heart of a man is exalted; and before he be glorified, it is humbled."[54] "God hath abolished the memory of the proud, and hath preserved the memory of them that are humble in mind."[55]

How unworthy of divine benevolence is the mortal who, through his ambition for God's most signal blessings, perverts them into an obstacle to salvation.

[50] Prov. 16:5.
[51] James 4:6.
[52] Prov. 15:25.
[53] Ecclus. 10:17.
[54] Prov. 18:12.
[55] Ecclus. 10:21.

Chapter Seven

✑

Let God's favors
lead you closer to Him

How marvelously great was the message of the archangel! "Behold," said Gabriel, "thou shalt conceive in thy womb, and shalt bring forth a Son, and thou shalt call His name Jesus. He shall be great, and shall be called the Son of the Most High, and the Lord God shall give unto Him the throne of David His father; and He shall reign in the house of Jacob forever. And of His kingdom there shall be no end."[56] How well calculated was this message to inspire with excessive pride any child of Adam except Mary, whose self-extinction so endeared her to God!

How sublimely magnificent the promise: the Son of God shall be the Son of Mary. He shall sit, not on the material throne of David His father, but on a spiritual

[56] Luke 1:31-33.

throne of which David's was but the poorest symbol. Not merely shall He rule over the temporal interests of men, but His sovereign sway shall extend into regions where earthly monarchs dare not enter; His jurisdiction shall be over immortal souls made to the image and likeness of the Triune God. He shall change the face of the earth and be the Founder of Christian civilization. His kingdom shall witness the destruction of empire after empire; it shall behold dynasty after dynasty prostrate in the dust, because, like Him, its divine Founder, His kingdom shall be eternal: "Of His kingdom there shall be no end."

He shall reign over His true followers and shall lead them in the way of justice, holiness, and truth. He shall not teach the varying, unstable opinions of men, but shall herald forth to the whole earth the eternal truths of God's word. Under the energizing power of His teaching, men dreaming on in the world's slumber shall awake and be alive unto God.

"He shall be great, and shall be called the Son of the Most High." Immeasurably inferior will be the human, temporal grandeur of the kings of this world when compared with the divine, eternal glory of Him, the omnipotent Ruler of Heaven and earth, the King of kings and the Lord of lords.

Such was the burden of the mightiest message ever sent by God to man. The delicately sensitive and unspeakably humble Virgin, rapt in silent communion with her God, trembled at the words of the heavenly messenger. But Gabriel comforted her: "Fear not, Mary, for thou hast found grace with God."[57] Grace so great did she find with God by her humility that she was chosen to cooperate with His divine Son in restoring man to a dignity far superior to what he had lost by sin.

Her exaltation above all other creatures, described by the angel, failed to awaken within her impassioned thoughts, high aspirations, or sublime imaginings. She indulged no such luxury of feeling. Inwardly distressed and outwardly agitated by a message so mysterious, she was under the spell of the urgent persuasions of excited fear. She could not reconcile motherhood with virginity.

"How," she exclaims to the angelic envoy, "shall this be done, because I know not man?"[58] Mary's pertinent

[57] Luke 1:30.
[58] Luke 1:34.

question betrayed no distrust of the omnipotence of God. She was anxious, not indeed to pry into the secrets of God, but to reveal the human inconsistency that surprised and shocked her, the difficulty of squaring the observance of her vow with the divine maternity. The preservation of her virginity was her deep concern.

Severed as she was from the world of sense, her heart all impressed with a heavenly character, Mary — in her thoughts and her words — was completely under the influence of the supernatural, because of her constant, unswerving fidelity to grace. Her question was inspired by the Holy Spirit, and led the way to His further revelation when Gabriel apprised her of how her stupendous vocation would be accomplished. Full of grace as she was, her words did not proceed from any tendency to separate God's favors from His divine will, and to dwell on the former at the expense of the latter.

It is indeed a lesson we can never learn too well that it is not the most lavishly generous tokens of divine munificence, but the virtue issuing from our loving correspondence with His grace, that will enable us to give glory to our Creator and, thus, by making us ring true to the purpose of our creation, render our souls eternally precious in His sight.

The sacraments, for example, those masterpieces of divine ingenuity, were instituted not only to dower our souls with the riches of Heaven, but also to smooth for us the path of Christian righteousness so that we might run the way of God's commandments with enlarged hearts and with a joy that earth knows not. If they fail to detach us from the world, if they do not make us "labor for the meat which endureth unto life everlasting,"[59] if they do not annihilate our natural selves and make us ardent lovers of Christ crucified, they will be for us the means of our eternal condemnation.

But Mary did not need this lesson. Her esteem of virginity was not grounded in self-love but was the work of God Himself. And had she been wholly preoccupied with the contemplation of her ineffable prerogative, and forgetful of her earlier obligations as a result of her vow of virginity, God would not have selected her for the part that she played in the most memorable manifestation of love and mercy ever witnessed on earth.

[59] Cf. John 6:27.

Chapter Eight

⋈

Believe that nothing is impossible with God

The heavenly legate relieved Mary's distress of mind and directed her disturbed feelings into another channel with the comforting words: "The Holy Spirit shall come upon thee, and the power of the Most High shall over-shadow thee."[60] The Holy Spirit, he tells her, shall work in her the greatest work of His omnipotence. He shall depart from nature's laws and perform a prodigy that shall make even the angels mute with bewildered wonder. By His almighty power, He shall form and fashion the body of the Savior of the world, and the divine Son will unite it to Himself forever.

What an astounding manifestation of God's omnipotence is the accomplishment of this marvelous miracle!

[60] Luke 1:35.

All rational speculation on the overpowering mystery would necessarily range off into the twilight and darkness of the unknowable. Finite reason cannot explore the realm of this transcendental truth, so completely hidden from the limited eye and mind of man. Even the simple things of nature, enveloped as they are in divine mystery, baffle and confound human understanding. The more a mind trained to careful thinking tries to know the universe, the more conscious it becomes of its limitations and the more it realizes the mystery shrouded in darkness behind the phenomena, no matter how luminous, that reveal its existence.

Incomprehensible to men and angels, belief in so wondrous an exhibition of God's power demands of Mary an act of the most sublime faith. She naturally inquires into the achievement of the impenetrable mystery, and although Gabriel's answer is beyond her grasp, she opens her reason to the flooding light of faith and humbly submits to the power of Him who cannot be limited in His works by man's constricted mental horizon.

And oh, how God rewards the humble submission of her deep, living faith! "And therefore also," continues the archangel, "the Holy which shall be born of thee shall be called the Son of God."[61] He who shall be born of her shall be holy with the unutterable holiness of God, for His flesh shall be the flesh of the Son of God. His human soul and His human body will be substantially and indissolubly united to His divine nature so as to form one person, His soul and body being respectively the soul and body of God incarnate.

How becoming, then, it was that the Mother of the God-Man should have been immaculate from the first instant of her conception.

And wishing to demonstrate the consummate ease with which the Holy Spirit can perform this overwhelming miracle, the celestial messenger exclaims, "Behold thy cousin Elizabeth. She also hath conceived a son in her old age, and this is the sixth month with her that is called barren, because no word shall be impossible with God."[62] The Holy Spirit, who is God and hence the Author of nature and of nature's laws, can and shall, without changing these laws, suspend them by a single act of His all-powerful will.

[61] Luke 1:35.
[62] Luke 1:36-37.

❦

The lesson is self-evident. If God should choose a soul in which to accomplish an extraordinary work, He is in no way bound to enlighten the soul so that it may understand the means whereby the work will be accomplished. But He does condescend to ask that soul's generous correspondence with Him on grounds that, although incomprehensible, do not contravene finite reason and that must be accepted, because the motive of their credibility is the truthfulness and the infinite power of God.

It is, then, futile for us to try to forecast the crosses that God, in His wisdom and love, may see fit to send us; for, "Oh, the depth of the riches of the wisdom and of the knowledge of God! How incomprehensible are His judgments and how unsearchable His ways! For who hath known the mind of the Lord? Or who hath been His counselor?"[63]

Vain, too, it is for us to strive curiously to divine how He will enable us to bear them with absolute surrender of ourselves and thus to advance in the science of the saints and glorify Him whom all creation is bound to serve.

[63] Rom. 11:33-34.

"The just man liveth by faith."[64] "They that fear the Lord will not be incredulous to His word."[65]

Despite our senses and our arrogant reason, we must never doubt Him who cannot deceive and whose power is incomprehensible because it is infinite. When the exterior voice of the Church coincides with the interior voice of conscience, we are certain that God has spoken. We must, then, believe and obey.

[64] Rom. 1:17.
[65] Ecclus. 2:18.

∞

Chapter Nine

Recognize God's greatness and your littleness

Without any excitement or agitation — rather, with that lightness of spirit and activity of mind attending any release from suffering and constraint — and although not knowing the meaning of the archangel's inspired words, soothed by them to tranquillity and peace, Mary serenely submits to the will of God. In so doing, she utters the most gracious act of humility that ever fell from human lips: "Behold the handmaid of the Lord. Be it done to me according to thy word."[66]

Truths worthy of our absorbing study lie lurking under the Virgin's wholehearted conformity to the divine will.

First of all, God sent one of the highest ministers of His heavenly court to solicit the consent of her whom He

---

[66] Luke 1:38.

had chosen to be the mother of His divine Son. What courteous consideration of the creature! What divine deference to the will of man! God rules His rational creatures by love. He does not coerce them. On the contrary, He not only asks them to concur with Him in the accomplishment of His designs, but lovingly listens to their objections.

The ineffable dignity conferred on Mary demanded of her the greatest sanctity. Now, *sanctity* is only another name for suffering. "If any man will follow me, let him deny himself and take up his cross and follow me."[67] The divine motherhood meant for Mary sheer self-extinction through total abandonment to the will of God. It implied her acceptance of the bitterest suffering. It forecast mental pain that would almost consume her, its victim. To become the Mother of God augured for Mary a knowledge of and a share in the Passion of Christ that would plunge her into the depths of a sea of lonely desolation for souls and make the tempest overwhelm her.

Suffering being the measure and the very law of love, we cannot adequately conceive the height and depth, the

[67] Mark 8:34.

length and breadth of her love for us, her children. By becoming the Mother of God and our mother, Mary became a holocaust to the divine will, the Queen of Martyrs, the most perfect imitator of Him whom Lacordaire[68] has called "a Victim to be destroyed for sin, but a living and a dying Victim whose sacrifice was never interrupted, Jesus Christ."

To suffer so much, the Blessed Virgin supremely needed help from on high. This truth, worthy of our most serious thought, we are apt to overlook. It is peculiarly and essentially human to stress the sublimity of Mary's exaltation and forego entirely any reckoning of its awful price. To give to the world its Savior, it was imperative for Mary to exemplify, in magnificent terms, a supernatural heroism manifested by a spirit of self-sacrifice to which a careless, sensual, or unbelieving mind is alien. A mind destitute of the love and fear of God, with narrow views and earthly aims, a low standard of duty and a benighted conscience, a mind contented with itself and unresigned to God's will might be fascinated with the incomparable dignity of the Mother of God; but fascination

[68] Henri Dominique Lacordaire (1802-1861), French Dominican preacher.

with her dignity could not keep even such an obtuse soul from pained apprehension of the withering sorrow associated with her acceptance of that dignity. To become the Mother of Christ, Mary had to drain with Him the bitter chalice of His Passion to its very dregs. It meant for her virtually the annihilation of nature.

For Mary to endure such suffering, her virtue had to be built on the rock of humility. The immeasurable humility of the Mother of God is a truth whose content is inexhaustible.

The very moment of her exaltation, the highest to which God could raise a creature, finds her sunk in the abyss of her own nothingness and exclaiming to the archangel, "Behold the handmaid of the Lord." Thus fully acknowledging her unworthiness to be the Mother of Christ, she accepts the inestimable privilege only in obedience to the divine will: "Be it done to me according to thy word." At the very apex of her glory, not her elevation above all other creatures, but her own nothingness, absorbs her. She calls herself the servant of Him who for thirty years will be subject to her. She receives God's greatest gift in perfect accord with the mind of the divine Donor.

∽

What a lesson in humility Mary teaches us! Too often the reception of God's gifts ministers to our self-love and vanity, whereas the abiding conviction of our unworthiness to receive them — and this alone — constitutes our true greatness in His sight.

Chapter Ten

∾

Ponder God's wisdom as Mary did

In the simplest language, St. John announces the most important fact of history. "The Word was made flesh," says the Apostle of Love, "and dwelt among us."[69] The instant that Mary gave her consent to the archangel, the Holy Spirit overshadowed her and wrought in her most chaste womb the Incarnation of the Son of God.

The humble Virgin is absolutely silent on the subject of this stupendous miracle wrought within her by the divine power, this mystery incomprehensible even to the angels. Nor does she speak of the rapturous heavenly joy that floods her pure soul.

Such silence, born of the inspiration of the Holy Spirit and the conviction of one's own nothingness, and appealing to us with the eloquence of God, should be the

---

[69] John 1:14.

divine principle of our conduct when God favors us with His extraordinary graces. When conscious of these wondrous communications, we should reveal them only to our spiritual director. He will tell us whether they have any ecclesiastical or scriptural warrant or whether they are the work of the foul enemy of souls. Christ warns us to "beware of false prophets"[70]; and St. John says to us, "Believe not every spirit, but try the spirits, if they be of God."[71]

As we are not sufficient of ourselves, we should not even reflect on these rare revelations, much less analyze their effect. We are so permeated with self-love that we unfortunately yearn for whatever will foster it. Thus, instead of gaining power over ourselves by allowing these unique graces to flow freely into our souls without curious investigation of their reason, we neutralize, through pride, their divine influence and willingly succumb to temptations to vanity. Under the spell of this insidious vice, we compare ourselves to others much more advanced than

[70] Matt. 7:15.
[71] 1 John 4:1.

we in the way of God. We put ourselves on a level even with the saints and fruitlessly try to understand their close relationship with God, or we peruse authors who undertake to expound mysteries that demand adoration rather than discussion.

Holy Scripture does far otherwise, and in this respect, as in all others, it is our best teacher. Of the Fall, for example, the sacred writer only states, "She took of the fruit thereof, and did eat, and gave to her husband, who did eat."[72] Of the death eternal in its consequences, the volume of inspiration merely records, "They crucified Him."[73]

Vain curiosity springing from intellectual pride so contracts the mind and soul as to render them incapable even of investigating, not to speak of maintaining, divine truth. God's revelation is not meant to pander to our self-love and our self-conceit. Here, we live by faith; hereafter, God will lift the veil and we shall know even as we are known.[74] Too meticulous an examination of what we must believe on the authority of God argues a woeful lack

[72] Gen. 3:6.
[73] Mark 15:25.
[74] Cf. 1 Cor. 13:12.

of faith. For the just man, it is enough that God has spoken, because "the just man liveth by faith."[75] The saints raised themselves to their high estate of holiness, not by the searching scrutiny of God's truth, but by squaring their lives with it. They were "wise unto sobriety."[76]

If we are to follow in their footsteps, we must not delve into the secrets of Divine Revelation, but must practice what it teaches. To do this, we must mortify ourselves. The Devil, who is a consummate strategist, knows with the intelligence of an angel how powerful an ally he has in our loathsome self-love. At times he beguiles a person with the fatal delusion that, to become a saint, he must do the extraordinary. Once he has indoctrinated the person with this falsehood, he inspires him to read authors who present their own false notions instead of the true doctrine of the masters of the spiritual life. And so they blind him with vanity in order that the beauty of holiness may no longer attract him, and, in a moment of petulance and despondency, yielding to

[75] Rom. 1:17.
[76] Rom. 12:3.

discouragement, he convinces himself that the pursuit
of sanctity is wearisome, the yoke of the Lord galling, and
His burden intolerable.

Mary teaches us how to overcome this subtle temptation. Her wisdom kept pace with her humility. She could truthfully say, "I make doctrine to shine forth to all as the morning light, and I will declare it afar off. I will penetrate to all the lower parts of the earth, and will behold all that sleep, and will enlighten all that hope in the Lord. I will yet pour out doctrine as prophecy, and will leave it to them that seek wisdom, and will not cease to instruct their offspring even to the holy age."[77] Mary surpassed all others in wisdom, because her intimate union with Christ was the measure and sum of her enlightenment. She is truly the Seat of Wisdom, because she was the living tabernacle of the God of infinite wisdom.

"But Mary kept all these words, pondering them in her heart."[78] And oh, how impressive and efficacious was her eloquence of silence! By her remarkable and reverent reserve, she did more to "make doctrine shine forth to all

[77] Ecclus. 24:44-46.
[78] Luke 2:19.

as the morning light" than she could have done by the most vivid revelation of the wonders that God had wrought within her and of the treasures of wisdom with which He had enriched her.

Chapter Eleven

Be attentive to God's presence within you

Conscious, after having received Christ, of being rooted in her God, Mary possessed a sanctity characterized by a heavenly sublimity beyond understanding. She was not only full of grace, but she bore the Author of grace. She was wholly under the influence of Christ's divinity. In return for the natural strength that Mary gave Him, He invigorated her with His divine strength.

Marvelous interchange! Closest of all unions both naturally and supernaturally! Oh, the divine impress of Christ upon Mary, for both mother and Child are physically one! And they are morally one. Mary's thoughts and desires, then, are those of her divine Son. Her heart beats in unison with His heart.

So hardly won is every step in our Christian course, so supine and sluggish is our correspondence with grace, that we can form but a very vague and imperfect idea of the interior spirit of the mother of the incarnate Word during the period in which she physically possessed her God. Suffering the varying circumstances of every day to sway us, we would have to be entirely detached from the world to appreciate with any degree of accuracy her gift of prayer, both mental and vocal, while she was the living tabernacle of the eternal Word.

He who had become bone of her bones and flesh of her flesh was the divine principle of her life. In order to pray, she had no need of frequenting the Temple made with hands. The temple not made with hands — that is, her soul — was the most marvelous house of prayer ever created by God's omnipotence. The efficacy of Mary's prayer can be fully understood only through a complete comprehension of the intimacy of her union with her divine Son. Her prayer was the prayer of Christ.

Astounding mystery!
Thou, O God, who dwellest
in the bosom of the Father from all eternity,
dost condescend to repose in the chaste womb
of Thy mortal creature!

Transported with love, joy, and gratitude, St. Epiphanius[79] exclaims, "Hail, full of grace, thou who art the golden urn containing the manna from Heaven!"

We cannot rise to the lofty heights of Mary's holiness, because we cannot grasp the intimacy of her union with Christ when she became His mother. But we can discover the reason her sanctity soared higher and higher during the time Christ dwelt within her.

Mary had conceived Christ by her humility: "He hath regarded the humility of His handmaid."[80] On becoming the Mother of the God-Man, she stifled all thought of herself, for she was so absorbed with the contemplation of her God that she could think only of Him. Now that He had taken up His abode within her, He enlightened her to understand, as she never had or could heretofore, the greatness of God and the nothingness of man. He taught her that the eternal Father could be adequately adored and praised, propitiated and thanked, only by the inconceivable humiliations of a God made man. With her mind thus illumined with divine light, she realized

---

[79] St. Epiphanius (c. 315-403), Bishop of Salamis.
[80] Luke 1:48.

that her homage was of itself valueless, not even worthy of acceptance.

Having learned the lesson of humility perfectly, Mary disappeared from her own eyes and glorified God through her divine Son. She was lost in the ocean of infinity within her. Bearing the Savior annihilated for sinners, she effaced herself entirely. As we cannot measure the depths of her humility, we can have no true notion of her spiritual exaltation.

Self-knowledge is at the root of all real growth in holiness. We can no more advance in the path of sanctity without humility than we can live without air.

Humility is the heart and soul of virtue. It is humility that gives power and efficacy to all we do for God. The fact that Christ became "a worm, and no man, the reproach of men and the outcast of the people"[81] in order to teach us humility impressively proves the absolute necessity of this fundamental virtue in the divine economy of salvation. To imbibe in the largest measure the power and fullness of God's Spirit, we must imitate

---

[81] Ps. 21:7 (RSV = Ps. 22:6).

Christ, who, "to seek and to save that which was lost,"[82] "emptied Himself."[83] Without humility, we cannot bring ourselves into the remotest resemblance to our Savior or even to Mary, whose humility not only merited for her the surpassing dignity of Mother of God, but actually made her His mother.

If, through pride, we become destitute of every element of attractiveness that wins the acceptance of men, what objects of detestation pride must make us in the sight of God, who, to inculcate — even more, to make us ardently love — humility, the indispensable virtue, took "the form of a servant"[84] by clothing Himself with our frail flesh, becoming like us in all things but sin and dying in our fallen nature.

O wondrous, incomparable humility! Without thee, we live only under the shadow and enjoy merely the name of Christian, and we will never partake of its future blessedness.

Proud preference of self is uncompromising opposition to God. Pride puts us out of the pale of God's mercy,

[82] Luke 19:10.
[83] Phil. 2:7.
[84] Ibid.

for "God resisteth the proud."[85] Therefore, let us, like Mary, realize our nothingness. Then God will flood our souls with grace here and will exalt them eternally hereafter.

[85] 1 Pet. 5:5.

Chapter Twelve

Bring Christ to others

Informed by the archangel that St. Elizabeth would soon become a mother, Mary, with her mind enlightened, her sympathies quickened, and her heart on fire with divine charity, hastened to visit her cousin in order to congratulate and serve her. But God's ultimate purpose, although unknown to the humble Virgin, was to sanctify, by the visit of His mother, His great precursor and thus to prepare him for his unique mission.

Most fruitful of salutary lessons is this long, fatiguing journey of the Mother of God. With what consummate grandeur does Mary thereby hold mirrored before us her distinctive virtue: humility! Had she followed the persuasions of human reason, she would have tendered both her congratulations and her services through an intermediary, because, although much younger than her cousin, she was inestimably superior to her in dignity. Impelled by natural inclinations, Mary, realizing her pre-eminence among men and angels, would have considered such a visit at variance with the majesty and sublimity of her high estate. But she was too thoroughly grounded in humility to entertain so proud a thought. This virtue, her chief glory, made the visit her duty.

It was the archangel, not Elizabeth, who informed her of her cousin's condition. Yet Mary was not influenced by human motives, which, in view of this fact, would have rightly concluded that her cousin would not be offended by her failure to visit her. Nor, on the other hand, was she in the least disturbed because Elizabeth had not told her that she was an expectant mother. Mary's visit, like every other act of her life, was inspired by the supernatural. Her humility, rising above the natural, made the long, hard journey a mission of love.

If we profess to be true children of our heavenly mother, we will not yield to our natural desires, but will ever follow the promptings of grace. We will then discharge every duty, no matter how insignificant, to our neighbor. To be negligent in this respect is to have a distorted notion of piety. While true religion forbids idle gossip with the world, it commands us to pay due regard to the ties of relationship and to the canons of civility. Devotion suffers only by forgetfulness of God and of our neighbor. Mary, during her difficult and painful journey, forgot herself entirely and thought only of God and of her cousin, the image of God.

In our following the inspirations of grace, purity of intention, which makes God the beginning and the end of all our activity, is bound to animate us. Divine Providence often uses our human contacts for a supernatural end. For the soul wholly under the dominion of the spiritual, every slightest task and duty is of notable import even though the designs of God are completely hidden.

To the superficial observer, the visit of Mary to her cousin may seem a very ordinary event in her life. But how momentous it was to God the Father, who, through the presence of His most favored daughter, wished to sanctify the precursor of His divine Son! Although not knowing the mind of God in this eventful visit, Mary, under the quickening power of grace, was a most willing instrument in the execution of His designs. Had she not followed the urgings of grace, she would have frustrated the divine plan.

∞

This truth has a practical bearing. An apparently commonplace circumstance in our lives may be the means of the salvation of our neighbor. Although, for the moment, we cannot see the connection between our conduct and this effect, we should at least divine its possibility. We must therefore make our social interchanges something more than the satisfaction of the forms prescribed by polite society.

Limitless are our opportunities for doing good in this world's wilderness of sin. In our daily relationships, we are unconsciously influencing our fellowmen. This is a fearful responsibility and one we cannot escape. We can change the course of a life by a kind word or a generous deed; by our example, we can lead souls either to Heaven or to Hell. We profess to be followers of Christ, but the test of our discipleship is practical charity — that is, the diffusion of the good odor of Christ in our daily dealings with others.

Although frail, dependent mortals, weak vessels of clay, what mighty moral powers we are! How unspeakable in magnitude, how far-reaching, and how lasting, under the guidance of grace, is our influence for good! What food we can, by the power of our example, furnish to souls spiritually starving! If we live what we believe, if we labor solely for the honor and glory of God, if, in short, we are God's devoted creatures, we will enrich and ennoble with our heavenly store every mortal whose life we touch.

Chapter Thirteen

∽

Rely on faith in the face of doubt

How telling was the meeting of the Mother of God and the mother of St. John! What prodigies Christ wrought through Mary's colloquy with Elizabeth! With no visible disclosure of His divine action, He freed His precursor from Original Sin, enriched him with grace, and made him leap with joy at the sound of Mary's voice: "And it came to pass that when Elizabeth heard the salutation of Mary, the infant leaped in her womb."[86]

The mother of His herald He simultaneously filled with His Holy Spirit and made her understand the reason for her child's ecstasy. In the veiled presence of her God, Elizabeth confessed that Mary was the Mother of Christ: "And Elizabeth was filled with the Holy Spirit. And she cried out with a loud voice and said, 'Blessed art thou

[86] Luke 1:41.

among women, and blessed is the fruit of thy womb.' "[87]
She declared Mary blessed among women because Mary
was the most holy dwelling of the eternal God, Christ
our Lord. All this Elizabeth had learned from the child
she was bearing, who, in turn, was taught by the Word
incarnate in the womb of Mary.

What tremendous significance, then, God attached
to what appeared to be an ordinary visit demanded by
the laws of propriety and courtesy!

Lovingly docile to God's will, Mary was the victim
not of pained but of joyous surprise when she discovered
that the Holy Spirit had revealed to Elizabeth what she
had resolved to keep a secret between herself and God.
Not knowing that the divine Child within her had illumined St. John, the Blessed Mother was at a loss to discover how her cousin had acquired her information.
Elizabeth's open profession of faith followed when, inspired by the Holy Spirit, she exclaimed, "Whence is this
to me, that the Mother of my Lord should come to me?"[88]
Thus did she establish the reality of the amazing favor

---

[87] Luke 1:41-42.
[88] Luke 1:43.

that God had conferred on Mary. The humble Virgin did not ask for its confirmation, but God gave it to her when she had least expected it.

Full of meaning is this phase of Mary's life for the one whom God directs in an extraordinary way. Often diffidence of self issuing from doubt about his interior state follows or even coexists with such a person's abandonment to Divine Providence. This is due either to a gradual weakening of his first fervor or to the wiles of Satan, who throws his soul into a turmoil by focusing its vision too inordinately on its internal condition. In his perplexity, the person should not ask for a sign from Heaven, but, with filial trust in God, should await the divine comfort with which God will allay his fears and dispel his anxiety at the time best suited to further his spiritual progress.

God will never forsake one who needs His help. In the person's distress, God will initiate him by degrees into a clear understanding of the workings of grace within his soul. When God does not condescend to satisfy his yearning to hear His voice, that person must intensify his faith and blindly obey his spiritual director.

Were God to speak whenever he desired, He would only accentuate his own self-sufficiency and thus drive him far from Him. Mary, being dead to herself, never longed for God to speak to her until He deemed it necessary for the accomplishment of His designs in her regard.

It is Mary's intense faith that Elizabeth blesses, for she says to her, "And blessed art thou that hast believed, because those things shall be accomplished that were spoken to thee by the Lord."[89] How she would be a mother and at the same time remain a virgin did not enter into the equation of Mary's faith. She implicitly believed the word of God as announced to her by His messenger.

God always rewards strong faith lavishly. It is the sign of the highest virtue to retain belief unshaken when agonizing doubts strive to weaken its initial strength. But it is the most convincing evidence of the faith that moves mountains to continue to believe most firmly when God appears to work for the frustration of His plans or when difficulties arise apparently contradicting His original revelation.

[89] Luke 1:45.

A comparison between the message of Gabriel predicting the greatness and the glory of Christ, and the life of the Redeemer Himself, categorically proves the strength of Mary's faith. The Savior was the poorest of the children of men. He was born into His own world homeless. In the workshop of an unknown and humble carpenter, He toiled in obscurity for thirty years. In His public life, He had nothing — neither money nor even a place to lay His head.[90] He depended for support on the uncertain charity of those to whom He ministered so graciously. "I am poor," He tells us, "and in labors from my youth."[91]

He was the object of ridicule, scorn, and contempt. He was treated as a fool, branded as one who worked by the power of the Devil, and stigmatized as one possessed by the Devil. He was blindfolded, mocked, scourged, and spat upon. So relentless was the opposition, so implacable the hatred of His own people, that they released a public malefactor rather than Him, their God, while instead they crucified Him between two thieves.

[90] Cf. Matt. 8:20; Luke 9:58.
[91] Ps. 87:16 (RSV = Ps. 88:15).

How can we harmonize the hidden life and the public life of Christ with the glorious declaration of the archangel? The one seems to be a flat contradiction of the other. And yet Mary firmly believed the words of the heavenly messenger. How inconceivably strong her faith! And how munificently the eternal Father rewarded it by His divine Son's marvelous Resurrection and His eternal triumph over sin and death and all the powers of Hell!

Chapter Fourteen

&

Rejoice in God's greatness

Mary answers her cousin with a heavenly lyric. Divinely
eloquent, the humble Virgin exclaims, "My soul doth
magnify the Lord. And my spirit hath rejoiced in God my
Savior."[92] The rapturous joy that fills her heart throws her
into an ecstasy. We can have but a vague notion of her
happiness, the effect of the presence of the incarnate God
within her, which is for her a foretaste of the bliss of the
blessed. She is transported beyond herself. Yet she extols
the greatness of God and emphasizes her own nothingness; although glorified immeasurably beyond the angels,
because of her fidelity to grace, it is not her own but
God's glory for which her immaculate soul yearns.

Oh, how pleasing to God is this, His favored child!
The more He favors her, the more she praises His mercy

---

[92] Luke 1:46-47.

and disregards her own personal exaltation! How unlike
us is Mary!

So self-centered are we that we seek and esteem virtue
for its own sake, and not for the honor and glory of God.
The virus of our self-seeking poisons the wellsprings of
our spiritual life. How few of us can free ourselves from
the Satanic tyranny of our self-love! We desire God's
favors for our own individual gain, and not for our ad-
vancement in virtue and the consequent glorification
of their divine Donor. Mary's self-renunciation should
teach us how to overcome this deadly vice, even though
the price of victory is for us, as it was for her, moral
crucifixion.

The fact that God has condescended to regard her is
the sole reason for her overwhelming joy: "My spirit hath
rejoiced in God my Savior, because He hath regarded the
humility of His handmaid."[93] She fully realizes that she is
God's debtor, because she is wholly convinced of her own
nothingness. Although she is the Mother of Christ, she
calls herself His handmaid. Because we fail to recognize
our nothingness and indulge pride, God turns from us.

[93] Luke 1:47-48.

Were He to look on us, His divine glance would serve only to deepen in us the worst of all vices.

Mary lays claim to greatness only through God's mercy. In divine accents, she pours out her soul: "From henceforth all generations shall call me blessed."[94] It is only because God has regarded her that all generations shall call her blessed. There is in her most pure soul not even a lingering suspicion of self-love.

Her humility is genuine because she praises God's favors with the conscious conviction of their greatness and of her unworthiness to receive them. "He that is mighty hath done great things to me; and holy is His name."[95] She lauds the omnipotence of God, who has but to command and nature obeys. It is His almighty power that evokes her tribute to His holiness: "Holy is His name." Only the good are supernaturally powerful. God being infinitely good, His power is necessarily unlimited. His works, therefore, are essentially good, and they are done for one end alone: the promotion of His glory. "Thou art worthy, O Lord, our God, to receive

[94] Luke 1:48.
[95] Luke 1:49.

glory and honor and power because Thou hast created all things."[96] Convinced of the obligation of gratitude, from which God cannot dispense His creatures, Mary returns the glory of His gifts to Him, their primal source, and keeps nothing for herself. Her dominant desire is to extol His power by glorifying His name and burying herself in her own nothingness. But God will raise her higher and higher in proportion to her self-effacement.

Only the humble seek the glory of God and thus render to Him what is His by divine right. It is a truth demonstrated by reason that all creation is bound to serve and thereby glorify the Creator. The law of service is the basic law of creation.

It is through serving God faithfully that man becomes the beneficiary of his Creator's mercy. How logical, then, is Mary when, continuing the sublime strains of her inspired lyric, she cries out: "His mercy is from generation unto generations to them that fear Him."[97] Those who love God fear Him, and hence do not offend Him.

---

[96] Apoc. 4:11 (RSV = Rev. 4:11).
[97] Luke 1:50.

Now, the greatest offense against God is to rob Him of the glory that is essentially His. This we do when we seek our own glory. Pride is therefore the worst of sins. God so punishes this cursed vice, the source of all evil, that He deprives the proud of His mercies. The proud travel the broad highway to Hell.

Let us observe Mary's hatred of pride. How trenchant is her language when speaking of this detestable vice that created Hell! "He hath showed might in His arm; He hath scattered the proud in the conceit of their heart."[98] Only the eternal pains of Hell can indemnify God for the honor and glory of which the proud so unjustly rob Him.

With the greatest lucidity, Mary declares the dispensations of God's Providence in the punishment of the proud. "He hath put down the mighty from their seat and hath exalted the humble."[99] Nearest to God in Heaven are the humble; farthest from Him are the proud in Hell.

The realization of this startling truth will make us saints. Those who hunger for justice — that is, the humble

[98] Luke 1:51.
[99] Luke 1:52.

who "render to God the things that are God's"[100] and thus practice virtue in its broadest sense — are, both in time and in eternity, the objects of His predilection. The rich — that is, those who appropriate God's gifts to subserve their pride — will be impoverished forever.

As a reward for Mary's unfathomable humility, the ineffably significant promises made to Abraham and to his children will be verified by the coming of Christ, but only through her free cooperation. By the Incarnation of the Son of God, Abraham will become the father of the Christians of all nations, and together with them will be of the chosen race of the Redeemer: "He hath received Israel, His servant, being mindful of His mercy. As He spoke to our fathers, to Abraham, and to his seed forever."[101]

Mary's *Magnificat*, inspired by Christ incarnate within her and spoken by her with all the heavenly magnificence of consummate artistry, is the most eloquent sermon ever preached on the fundamental virtue of Christianity. May we learn its lesson: the greatness of God and the nothingness of man!

[100]Cf. Matt. 22:21.
[101]Luke 1:54-55.

Chapter Fifteen

Bear yourself toward others as Mary did

It is very likely that the Blessed Virgin did not leave Elizabeth and return to Nazareth until after the birth of St. John the Baptist. Having fulfilled her mission to her cousin, her fine sense of delicacy impelled her to depart for home.

But what marvels she saw and heard during the three months she abode with the mother of the great precursor! She joyously listened to the spirited discussion about the name to be given to the Baptist; she heard the account of the vision vouchsafed to Zachary and of his punishment for doubting the angel who had informed him that his wife, although advanced in years, would give birth to a son. She witnessed the miraculous restoration of the patriarch's speech and heard his eloquent panegyric on the mercy of God and on the supreme dignity of his child, the herald of the Redeemer.[102] Thus she received, although unsolicited, a very remarkable confirmation of her own exalted state.

Who can estimate the degree of grace conferred on Elizabeth through daily contact with the Mother of God? Fraternal charity alone actuated Mary's visit. Bearing in her chaste womb the Creator of men and the Lord of angels, she infused blessings of the highest spiritual order into the soul of her virtuous relative, not only by her words and actions, but, by her mere presence. The house of Elizabeth, under the blessed influence of Mary, became a school of perfect sanctity in which everything was said and done from religious principle, thus enabling the mother of the Baptist to progress in holiness and allowing the virtues of Christ's precursor to develop to an extent that would verify the words of the Redeemer: "Amongst those that are born of women, there is not a greater prophet than John the Baptist."[103]

Nor did Mary's recollectedness suffer under her cousin's roof. True, she could not devote as much time to formal

[102]Cf. Luke 1:5-25, 57-79.
[103]Luke 7:28.

prayer as she did in the solitude of her home in Nazareth; but this did not interrupt her interior communion with her divine Son or change the tenor of her conversation, which always turned to God or the things of God. And so the house of Zachary and Elizabeth was, through the sanctifying presence of Mary, a house of prayer. By her exquisite, thoughtful charity, by the angelic sweetness of her manner, she fascinated them with the radiant beauty of her virtues, and thereby deepened and purified their own holiness, making the home of her honored relatives a veritable paradise of spiritual delights.

Far too often in our social dealings, we forego the duties while retaining the privileges of our Christian profession. From Mary's example, we should learn to value solitude, but when duties prescribed by custom and courtesy, indicating the will of God to us, reveal the opportune moment to serve our neighbor, we should willingly tender our services in a spirit of brotherly love.

Mutual edification characterized the interview of the Queen of Saints with her devout cousin. This teaches us ever to seek the company of the virtuous so that both we and they may advance in the way of perfection by the

reciprocal diffusion of the good odor of Christ. Since
man is a social being, fraternal charity is unquestionably
the touchstone of his moral worth. Man is veritably his
brother's keeper. Time is best spent, then, when it is
devoted to the spiritual welfare of our fellowmen.

Brotherly love must always be the inexorable law
of our relations with others. In our dealings with our
neighbor, we are at best only pagans if we dispense with
the claims of Christian charity: "By this shall all men
know that you are my disciples: if you have love one for
another."[104] Love of neighbor should always motivate
even our visits of courtesy, and we should not prolong
them after we have satisfied the demands of charity. Nor
should we mingle with others just to banish dissatisfac-
tion with ourselves. Such visits will only increase our
dissipation of mind.

We love God above all things only when charity is
the peremptory law of our social dealings. "Most saints
avoided as much as possible the company of men, and
chose to serve God in retirement. A pagan master has
said, 'As often as I have gone among men, I have returned

[104]John 13:35.

home less a man.'[105] This same thing we experience only too often when we have spent a long time in talking. It is easier to be altogether silent than not to exceed in words. It is easier to remain at home than to keep sufficient guard over oneself abroad. Whoever wishes to lead an interior life and to become spiritual must, with Jesus, keep aloof from the crowd."[106]

In this respect, what a perfect model for our imitation is the conduct of Mary. It would have been inconsiderate on her part to have left the house of Elizabeth before the birth of St. John the Baptist. To have prolonged her visit after his birth would have been equally out of place. As soon as she had fully discharged the duty of Christian charity to her cousin, she departed. Thereby she clearly taught us how to make our social life contribute to the sanctification of both ourselves and our neighbor.

[105]Lucius Annaeus Seneca (c. 4 B.C.-A.D. 65; Roman philosopher, dramatist, and statesman), *Letter 7*.

[106]St. Thomas à Kempis (c. 1380-1471; ascetical writer), *Imitation of Christ*, Bk. 1, ch. 20.

Chapter Sixteen

Remain serene even
when misunderstood

Mary's visit to Elizabeth occupied almost four months. On her return to Nazareth, her condition was very manifest to Joseph and naturally roused his suspicions. Ignorant of the message of the archangel and the succeeding miracles, he could not know that in permitting these very suspicions on his, Joseph's, part, the incarnate God was subjecting His Virgin Mother to one of the many pangs of her earthly martyrdom. Knowing that Mary had dedicated herself unreservedly to God by her vow of virginity and would not have espoused him unless he had solemnly pledged himself to respect it, and knowing his own fidelity in keeping his pledge, Joseph could not help but suspect, with the visible evidence before him, that she had sinned. His suffering was equal to the intensity of his affection for her whom he loved so ardently. Tortured

by agonizing doubt, he knew not what to do nor where
to turn.

While he maintained a holy silence, his countenance
mirrored the anguish that inwardly convulsed him. The
conviction that she was the blameless cause of his sharp
suffering oppressed the Immaculate Heart of Mary beyond
words. What a painful trial for these two favored creatures of God! Mary could have dispelled Joseph's doubts
and stilled the storm of his sensitive soul. Had she informed him of the miracle wrought within her, had she
narrated to him the wonders worked in the house of Elizabeth, he would have fallen down before her, the living
tabernacle of the eternal God.

But regardless of the consequences of silence, although
death might have been its penalty, she did not speak. Her
lips were sealed with a divine seal, because she was guard-
ing a divine secret. According to the law, Joseph could
have disgraced her before priests and people both, by
consigning her to an ignominious death for the crime
of which she seemed guilty.

Had Mary yielded to her natural inclination, she
would have spoken, to vindicate her character, to pacify
Joseph, and to defend the honor of God, which was so

inextricably bound up with her own. But she did not
utter a word. Wholly under the influence of the supernatural, she stifled all thought of self and kept an inviolate
silence, fully realizing in her profound humility that God
would reveal His own secret in His own time.

Oftentimes God's favors to us awaken the studied
hatred and cruel persecution of others. And frequently
we yearn to justify ourselves, almost entirely losing sight
of the eternal truth that "through many tribulations we
must enter into the kingdom of God."[107] In all such dis-
tressing trials, if we obey the promptings of self-love, we
seek to exonerate ourselves, at least in order to conciliate
our tormentors. We reason that it is unjust to leave our
neighbor under a false impression and perhaps therefore
to scandalize him by allowing him to indulge his wrong
notions about God's goodness to us. This, we convince
ourselves, we are bound to avoid doing, not only to defend, but also to increase, the honor and glory of God.
All such false reasoning is born of our worst enemy in
the warfare for salvation: our self-love.

[107] Acts 14:21.

What a rebuke to this arch-enemy of our souls is found in the conduct of Mary! She kept a holy silence and calmly awaited her justification by God. In the stress of searching anguish, her soul was at peace. She used her trial to intensify her humility by extinguishing all thought of herself. No one knew better than Mary God's estimate of the fundamental virtue of Christianity. She thoroughly understood that, by dying to herself, she would contribute most to the honor and glory of God.

What a lesson for us! When, through the reception of God's favors, we are placed in a false light, we should rejoice that God has enabled us to overturn the idol of our self-love and thus to love Him above all things for His own love-worthy sake. In the trials most repugnant to our natural selves, when we are misunderstood, misrepresented, or calumniated, let us be silent and, like Jesus and Mary, make no attempt at justification. Perfect imitation of Christ and His Blessed Mother means only one thing: death to ourselves. The soul that is dead to itself has mastered the fine art of living.

Chapter Seventeen
∽

Bear your sufferings with Christ

Joseph's distress, which Mary felt keenly, did not rob her of her peace of soul. Nor was she in any way disturbed because God did not immediately vindicate her innocence. Far from resorting to legal measures against her, Joseph treated her with the utmost kindness. Although suspicion clouded his mind, Mary's virtue was too evident to justify him in invoking upon her the full penalty of the law. He still revered the angelic sanctity of his singular spouse, and following the inspiration of grace, he refrained from exposing her publicly. But in order to protect her reputation, as well as his own, he decided to put her away secretly.

Fully determined not to tarnish her good name and, at the same time, to defend himself from the imputation of complicity in her apparent guilt, he was about to proceed with his plan. But God, having tried and proved Joseph's virtue, came to his assistance in his hour of sorest need and changed his bitter sorrow into thrilling happiness. "While he thought on these things, behold, the angel of the Lord appeared to him in his sleep, saying, 'Joseph, son of David, fear not to take unto thee Mary thy wife, for that which is conceived in her is of the Holy Spirit. And she shall bring forth a Son, and thou shalt call His name Jesus, for He shall save His people from their sins.' "[108]

This overpowering disclosure dispelled with immeasurable joy the sorrow that had crushed the heart of Joseph. What a revelation to him that he was the spouse of her who was at once a spotless virgin and the Mother of God! He had schooled his mind, under the influence of grace, into a charitable and forbearing temper, and oh, how God rewarded him! Speechless gratitude welled up spontaneously from every fiber of his acutely sensitive nature. The depths of his holy feelings cannot be fathomed by human intelligence. He obeyed the command of the angel with unquestioning promptitude, for we are told, "Joseph, rising up from sleep, did as the angel of the Lord had commanded him and took unto him his

[108]Matt. 1:20-21.

wife."[109] We may infer, although Holy Scripture does not state it, that Joseph informed Mary of his vision in order to comfort her who had suffered desolation untold because, although supernaturally sympathetic with him in his blighting grief, she was unable to calm the agitation of his afflicted soul.

These two magnanimous saints, shaping their actions by God's will rather than by the rule of the world, had tasted the full bitterness of the most corroding sorrow. But how quickly the God of all consolation changed their anguish into the holiest supernal joy! Joseph's love for Mary now knew no bounds. Mary now revered Joseph's virtue more than ever, and the trial that would have hopelessly severed their union, had she preferred man's fallible judgment to God's unerring will, only served to strengthen it.

Our lives are filled with alternating joy and sorrow. Both contribute to the greater glory of God and the sanctification of our souls. In every painful circumstance of life's hard journey, if we are fully resigned to His will, He

[109] Matt. 1:24.

cannot forsake us, because of our union with Him, but
He will, with divine generosity, lighten our burden. Conformity to the divine will is the supreme goal of life. But,
alas, through fear of the world's judgment or expectation
of worldly advantage, we often do, not God's will, but
our own.

What a rebuke to our disloyalty, to our trampling un-
derfoot the substance and real excellence of religion, is
the conduct of Mary and Joseph! Abandonment to the
divine will was their one distinct rule of action. In accor-
dance with this truly Christian principle, Mary would not
reveal her divine secret to Joseph even though the revelation would have completely banished his suspicions;
and rather than contravene this principle, Joseph did not
question his saintly spouse. Thus did they glorify God by
resignation to His will, and He, in turn, made their virtue
shine forth with heavenly luster.

We cannot choose between joy and sorrow. We must
suffer because we are sinners. If, after the example of Mary
and Joseph, we are patient under trial, if we accept it in
the true Christian spirit by not longing to prevent or cur-
tail it, God will not fail to comfort us. "According to the
multitude of my sorrows in my heart, Thy comforts have

given joy to my soul."[110] "If I shall walk in the midst of tribulation, Thou wilt quicken me; and Thou hast stretched forth Thy hand against the wrath of my enemies; and Thy right hand hath saved me."[111]

The way of the Cross is the only pathway to peace of mind here and to eternal peace hereafter. The realization of this truth will help us to overcome our natural antipathy to life's sufferings. Only in the school of the Cross can we learn the truest wisdom, the knowledge of Jesus Christ and Him crucified: and "this is eternal life, that they may know Thee, the only true God, and Jesus Christ, whom Thou hast sent."[112] Now, to know Christ is to suffer with Christ, and to suffer with Christ is to reign with Him forever.

"Why, then, do you fear? Take up the cross which opens to you the way to the kingdom! In the Cross is salvation; in the Cross is life; in the Cross is protection against the enemy. In the Cross is infusion of heavenly sweetness; in the Cross is strength of heart; in the Cross is joy of spirit. In the Cross is the treasure of virtues; in

[110]Ps. 93:19 (RSV = Ps. 94:19).
[111]Ps. 137:7 (RSV = Ps. 138:7).
[112]John 17:3.

the Cross is perfection and holiness. There is no salvation of soul nor hope of eternal life, except in the Cross. Take up, therefore, your cross and follow Jesus, and you will enter into life everlasting."[113]

[113] *Imitation of Christ*, Bk. 2, ch. 12.

Chapter Eighteen

❧

Carry out God's will in your everyday tasks

To accomplish the prophecy that the Messiah would be born in Bethlehem, the city of David, God did not work a miracle, but made use of the edict of a pagan emperor.

Caesar Augustus, in order to apportion the taxation of his subjects justly, had determined that the whole world should be enrolled. The decree ordered every family to journey to the city or town of its ancestors. Judea being under the vast jurisdiction of Rome, "Joseph went up from Galilee, out of the city of Nazareth, into Judea, to the city of David, which is called Bethlehem, because he was of the house and family of David, to be enrolled with Mary, his espoused wife, who was with child."[114]

[114]Luke 2:4-5.

From a human angle, the edict of a pagan emperor and the birth of Christ were as far apart as the earth's two poles. But from God's point of view, they were very closely connected, because Divine Providence, through the decree of Caesar, brought about the birth of the divine Babe in Bethlehem and thus verified the words of the prophet: "And thou, Bethlehem Ephrata, art a little one among the thousands of Juda: out of thee shall He come forth unto me that is to be the Ruler in Israel; and His going forth is from the beginning, from the days of eternity."[115] What looked to be the mere whim of chance was the accomplishment of the infallible will of God. Following the inspiration of grace, Mary and Joseph, in obeying the emperor, indirectly obeyed God.

The conscious conviction of the Blessed Virgin and her chaste spouse that the decree of an idolatrous prince was the revelation of God's will, teaches us a very fundamental truth. Because we cannot understand the infinite action of God on His world, we often wrongly associate the element of chance with the designs of the Creator.

[115]Mic. 5:2.

But if we knew the mind of the Lord, if we were able to unravel the perplexing and puzzling interlacings of the manifold lines of His Providence, we would live by knowledge, not by faith.

In trying to understand so deep a mystery, then, we only waste time and impede our normal growth in holiness. Rather, let us conform to the divine will, which is the purpose of life. Human events are not due to chance. God either ordains or permits them. Although we cannot comprehend the working of God's will in the government of His creation, we are not therefore to divorce ourselves from Him by doing only our own will. Blind submission to the divine will in all things is unquestionably the touchstone of strong, living faith. Harmony is the great, universal law of creation.

Every circumstance of our lives, no matter how trivial, is connected with our salvation. The society in which we move, our earthly schemes, sickness and health, joy and sorrow — all promote or retard our progress in virtue. To convince ourselves of this ignored truth, we have but to look back over our lives. How often has good or evil followed from what we falsely considered an insignificant event in our worldly lot?

Accordingly, it is self-evident that God's will must be the compass of our lives in temporal no less than in spiritual concerns; otherwise we will never die to ourselves and live solely to God. We belong to Him absolutely and entirely. Upon our submission to His will, therefore, depends our salvation, and He will further our dearest interests only if we totally abandon ourselves to Him.

How important, then, is the lesson that Mary and Joseph inculcate by their obedience to the command of an earthly sovereign. Nazareth, where they dwelt, was, in the natural course of events, the town in which Christ should have been born. But they did not demand of God a miracle as indisputable proof that Bethlehem was the divinely chosen birthplace of the Messiah. They saw God's will in the ordinance of the emperor.

When we ask God to accomplish His will in our regard by extraordinary means, we are but gratifying our pride. In executing His will, God rarely deviates from the natural order. Hence, what presumption it is on our part to expect Him to do for us what He did for His Blessed Mother and St. Joseph only in extreme urgency.

After Christ, no one has taught as eloquently as Mary how we must act when God wills us to bear the Cross.

She was in destitute circumstances, and in her critical
condition, to travel to a distant and strange land, in winter, and without even the necessities of life for herself or
her Child, required an act of the highest moral courage.
But she murmured neither against God nor against the
edict of Caesar Augustus, although the divine will as
manifested by the decree of the civil ruler entailed for
her distressingly bitter suffering. She did not question the
designs of Providence, but hastened to accomplish them.
Nor did she complain because God had sent her a cross
entirely at variance with her wondrous dignity as Mother
of Christ. Her confidence in God matched her love of
Him, and she departed calmly to seek a home among
strangers for the Creator of the world, her soul enrap-
tured with the peace of God.

Chapter Nineteen

✃

Love God for His own sake

The narrative of Christ's birth, inexhaustible in its meaning, is sublime in its simplicity. "While all things were in quiet silence and the night was in the midst of her course, Thy almighty Word leapt down from . . . Thy royal throne."[116] The Son of God, born miraculously of the Virgin Mary, is enthroned among the brute cattle. Only the faith of Mary could fully appreciate the utter destitution, the homelessness, of that eternally significant birth.

We can picture her lovingly embracing her Child and adoring Him as her God. We can visualize her wrapping Him in swaddling clothes and gently laying Him on the straw in the manger.

When we ponder the extreme poverty of the Child and the fact that, at His birth, there were only two

[116]Wisd. 18:14-15.

spectators, we cannot but marvel at the faith of His mother. Is this the God who "laid the foundations of the earth, when the morning stars praised Him together, and all the sons of God made a joyful melody"?[117] Cribbed and confined in the narrow manger, is this the God whom the heaven of heavens cannot contain? How can we reconcile the poverty and humility of His birth with the prophecy of the archangel that He would be great and would be called the Son of the Most High?

Reason, powerless before this overwhelming mystery, can only wonder and adore. The God "with whom there is no change nor shadow of alteration"[118] is now subject to the suffering of frail mortals. The God of infinite power is now a helpless Infant. Externally, He is like every other child. He knows all things, since He is God; but He cannot even speak, let alone communicate His knowledge intelligently. His inarticulate cries prove His helplessness.

How severely the eternal Father tried the faith of the mother of His divine Son! We cannot comprehend Mary's thoughts as she gazed on her Child with wondering awe.

[117]Cf. Job 38:4, 7.
[118]James 1:17.

How conflicting her feelings when she contemplated her own nothingness and the infinite greatness of the God miraculously born of her! Who can conceive the fervor of her prayer, the depths of her love, or the tenderness of her motherly solicitude?

Nor can we form a true idea of the peace and joy that Christ, with boundless beneficence, bestowed upon His mother. It was for Mary Heaven by anticipation when she lifted Him from the manger, cradled Him in her arms, or folded Him to her heart. Her happiness was indescribable when the body of her Child touched her body. That same body touches ours in Holy Communion. The love that Christ lavished upon His mother was not the love of an ordinary child. It was the product of reason and grace; it was divine love, not instinctive human love. And Mary received it with the utmost humility, never for a moment deeming herself worthy of it, but returning the glory of a favor so precious to her divine Benefactor.

Such love set her heart on fire with love of her infant Son. Not merely as her Son, but as her God, as her unique Savior, since she had shared anticipatively in the merits of His Passion and death, did the Blessed Mother love her divine Child. She fully appreciated that she could not love Him too much, because, as God, He was worthy of infinite love. Her love, actuated by grace, was purely supernatural. Its action, its fervor, and its progress could be neither diminished nor restrained, because Mary loved her Child and her God according to the measure of the grace with which she was full. We have but a very faint notion of the deluge of delight that overflowed unimpeded in her immaculate soul.

The love of her divine Child, which was the reason for Mary's indefinable joy, was also the cause of her bitter sorrow. The sword of sorrow that transfixed the heart of Christ likewise pierced her own heart. Mary's suffering equaled her love. But although both gripped her soul simultaneously, neither the one nor the other could disturb her peace of mind or victimize her with any inordinate thought of self. Her joy did not transport her, nor did her sorrow and suffering depress her. She received both with perfect resignation to the divine will.

Like Mary, we should strive with every power within us to love Christ for His own sake. Purity of intention will then characterize our thoughts, words, and actions. Our Lord will be their principle and term. "He who is perfect in charity," says St. Clement of Alexandria, "does not go through the motive of the love of God: God is the most important, nay, the only end of all the works of the lover."[119]

Love of God for His own sake is not mercenary. "It does not," to use the words of St. Bernard, "seek its own interests. True love suffices to itself; it is its own reward: it seeks nothing but the object beloved."[120] Again, like Mary, we should not long for divine comfort, but should willingly accept and bear the Cross in the spirit of true followers of our crucified Master.

[119]St. Clement of Alexandria (c. 150-c. 215; theologian), *Book of Stromata.*
[120]*Sermon on Canticles.*

Chapter Twenty

∽

Strive to be detached from worldly things

The views of worldly wisdom and the Providence of God are entirely incompatible.

In announcing the momentous fact of Christ's birth, the angel told the humble shepherds that they would recognize the Savior of the world by His poverty: "This day is born to you a Savior, who is Christ the Lord, in the city of David. And this shall be a sign unto you: You shall find the Infant wrapped in swaddling clothes and laid in a manger."[121] The eternal Father tested the faith of these illiterate men, but only to strengthen it; for immediately after the angel had conveyed his remarkable news to them, the celestial choirs chanted the most sublime symphony of the sweetest song that man ever heard: "Glory

[121]Luke 2:11-12.

to God in the highest, and on earth peace to men of good will."[122]

The shepherds proceeded at once to verify the heavenly revelation. With the disappearance of the vision, unable to restrain their feelings, they said to one another, " 'Let us go over to Bethlehem, and let us see this word that is come to pass, which the Lord hath showed to us.' And they came with haste, and they found Mary and Joseph, and the Infant lying in the manger."[123]

Simple and beautiful must have been their description of the remarkable illumination with which they had been so specially favored. We can behold them kneeling before the crib and adoring, praising, and thanking God, and paying their tribute of reverent homage and deep love to His mother. They could not but conclude that Christ had been born mysteriously, for they found Mary, not the victim of the painful suffering usually associated with childbirth, but in perfect health.

Her soul was doubtless stirred with sentiments of admiration for the wondrous Providence of God when she

[122]Luke 2:14.
[123]Luke 2:15-16.

witnessed the first adorers of her divine Child who had
been led to the crib by the message of an angel, and her
heart pulsed with gratitude for the high honor that God
had conferred on her. Never had she realized so vividly
God's estimate of poverty, humility, and simplicity; for
not to Herod and his sycophants, not to the rich and
powerful, not to the learned masters in Israel, not to the
proud and carnal-minded, but to the lowly and poor of an
outlying rural region was the astounding fact of Christ's
birth first revealed. In reflecting on this inspiring, soul-
stirring truth, Mary fully appreciated the meaning of her
own abject poverty and the extreme destitution of her
spouse.

Holy Scripture does not enlarge on the meeting of
Mary and the shepherds. It simply states, "Mary kept all
these words, pondering them in her heart."[124] She was too
well grounded in virtue to neglect any opportunity of advancing in the way of God. She lived only to glorify God
by her growth in holiness. Queen of Saints that she was,
she listened most attentively to the simple and appealing
message of the shepherds, which was inspired by the God

[124]Luke 2:19.

who had miraculously led these humble and sincere men to the lowly palace of the newborn King. "Pondering them in her heart," she used all their words for her spiritual nourishment.

How full of instruction for us is the revelation of Christ's birth to the poor and unassuming shepherds! Like them, we shall find Christ only if we are simple, guileless, humble, and docile. "Amen, I say to you, unless you be converted and become as little children, you shall not enter into the kingdom of Heaven."[125]

Only when the soul is innocent and artless, open and ingenuous, frank and confiding, does it become fit soil for the growth of every virtue. Childlike simplicity is the primeval novitiate of holiness. The searching rays of divine grace penetrate with the utmost ease the soul of a child. By becoming like little children in the sight of God, we will travel the path of perfection with giant strides, because the humility of the child is the most potent antidote against pride, whose deadening effect paralyzes our progress.

[125]Matt. 18:3.

Every phase of Christ's life is an object lesson portraying some particular truth. The angel informed the shepherds that they would find the Child wrapped in swaddling clothes. What could be more weak than a newborn infant thus attired! By willingly submitting to a state of extreme feebleness and therefore of total dependence, Christ taught us how to overcome the degrading bondage of our self-will, which makes us the worst of slaves. Perhaps we have learned in the school of bitter experience how prone we are to vice and how apathetic to virtue. "All men are ruined on the side of their natural propensities."[126] We must conquer our natural impulses if we do not wish to defeat eternally the designs of God in our regard.

Now, the human will is disciplined and reduced to a state of spiritual bondage by the virtue of obedience. As the infant Christ, wrapped in swaddling clothes, was incapable either of movement or resistance, but was wholly dependent upon His mother, so the soul, even though strong in faith, is spiritually inert and helpless. It becomes spiritually active through prompt obedience to lawful

[126]Cf. Edmund Burke, *Two Letters on the Proposals for Peace with the Regicide Directory*.

authority, especially to him who is for it the direct voice of God: its spiritual guide.

The soul interiorly mortified by fidelity in obeying the divine bidding as expressed to it by its director, finds it comparatively easy to practice the humility, the poverty, and the self-denial that Christ preaches with magic persuasiveness from His pulpit — the cheerless crib. How low He sank in the estimation of men in order to teach us the virtue that we must learn and practice before we can practice any other virtue!

In imitation of His overwhelming humility, we should never desire worldly honor and pre-eminence. "You know that the princes of the Gentiles lord it over them; and they that are greater exercise power upon them. It shall not be so among you, but whosoever will be the greater among you, let him be your minister. And he that will be first among you shall be your servant."[127]

Although the poorest of God's poor, if we are truly humble, we will not complain about the adverse conditions of our earthly lot. If rich, we will not glory in our abundance and make of it a dangerous, even fatal, gift,

[127]Matt. 20:25-27.

prompting us to indulge habits of luxury and indolence. On the contrary, we will be perpetually astir to alleviate human suffering and to improve the estate of God's favored children, the poor. By our spirit of detachment from riches, we will glorify God for His bounty and thus render ourselves impervious to the alluring appeal of sensuality. Disengagement from the perishable goods of earth will enable us to live mortified lives conformable to the doctrine and example of Jesus Christ. If we learn the lesson taught so forcefully by the eternal God from His comfortless crib, we cannot be delicate members of a crucified Head.

Chapter Twenty-One

ᴏ⩊

Embrace the Cross with Mary

Incarnate, Christ was not bound by human or positive law.
The lawgiver is not subject to his own laws, and Christ,
the God-Man, was the Lawgiver of both the old and the
new dispensations. But with a humility that shocks and
confounds our detestable pride, He freely submitted to
the rigorous and abasing ceremony of circumcision. Mary
beheld her Child, in subjecting Himself to this law,[128] sign
Himself with the sign of sinners and willingly accept the
punishment of their sin. She thus witnessed her divine
Son bind Himself to obey perfectly every ordinance of the
Old Law and offer Himself to His eternal Father as the
Victim of the New Testament for the sins of mankind.

The first shedding of His blood was but the sorrowful
prelude to its full outpouring on the heights of Calvary.

[128]Gen. 17:10.

Today, the storm is threatening, "for the sky is red and lowering."[129] On Golgotha, it will break with full force, when Christ will redeem man "from the curse of the Law, being made a curse for us, for it is written: Cursed is everyone that hangeth on a tree."[130]

If we could sound the depths of Mary's love for her Child, only then would we understand the anguish of her sorrow as she minutely observed the knife cutting his virginal flesh and the blood flowing from His sacred body.

But she docilely underwent this trial, the ominous foreboding of far greater pain, when she would, with her divine Son, drain the chalice of His Passion. With unshaken faith, she adored the decrees of Heaven, suffering as no other mother ever suffered or ever will. Through a common bond of sympathy born of most intense love for her Child, she became a holocaust with Him for the innumerable sins of men. Although her foresight of suffering, which began when she consented to be the Mother of Christ, intensified during this initial shedding of His blood, with the generosity characteristic of supernatural

[129]Matt. 16:3.
[130]Gal. 3:13.

sacrificial love, she united her offering of herself with that of her divine Son. Her faith, which was her love in action, enabled her to surrender herself to a life of perennial suffering with loving resignation to the will of God.

The name *Jesus* signifies "God is salvation, the Savior." Mary's foreknowledge of the Passion and death of Christ, consequent upon her free acceptance of the divine motherhood, enlightened her to understand the full meaning of this name, which her Child was called both at His circumcision and also by the angel before He was conceived in the womb. Of all mortals, she could best appreciate the sorrow and desolation identified with the name of her divine Son. Every time she uttered it, she felt, with a sorrow "great as the sea"[131] the agony and dereliction of His bitter Passion and His brutal Crucifixion; she realized that, although she was exalted to the highest heavens as Mother of God, her very exaltation would be the reason and the measure of her suffering. Christ, by His baptism of blood, became the King of martyrs; Mary, by sharing in spirit His Passion, became the Queen of Martyrs.

[131]Lam. 2:13.

❧

Can we claim Jesus as our blood Brother and Mary as our mother if we shrink from sorrow and pain? The Cross is inescapable. There is no salvation of soul nor hope of eternal life except in the Cross.

Take up your cross, therefore, and follow Jesus, and you will enter into life everlasting. He has gone before you carrying His Cross, and has died for you on the Cross, so that you also might carry your cross and desire to die on the cross. "If we be dead with Christ . . . we shall live also together with Christ."[132] "As you are partakers of the sufferings, so shall you be also of the consolation."[133]

"Behold, all depends on the Cross and dying on the Cross; and there is no other way to life and to true interior peace than the way of the holy Cross. . . . Go where you will, seek what you will, and you shall not find a higher way above, nor a safer way below, than the way of the holy Cross. Arrange all things to your liking, yet you shall always find something to suffer, whether you will it or not; and thus you will always find the Cross."[134]

[132] Rom. 6:8.
[133] 2 Cor. 1:7.
[134] *Imitation of Christ*, Bk. 2, ch. 12.

The patient endurance of life's hardships, in imitation of Jesus and Mary, is the price of eternal life. "Dearly beloved, think not strange the burning heat which is to try you, as if some new thing happened to you. But if you partake of the sufferings of Christ, rejoice that, when His glory shall be revealed, you may also be glad with exceeding joy."[135]

We must, then, appropriate the lesson of Christ's physical circumcision by the moral circumcision of our hearts, "the circumcision not made by hand in despoiling of the body of the flesh."[136] This is indispensable if we wish to resemble Christ and His Blessed Mother. Our yearning to become like to them will soften the pain of our earthly martyrdom, will make us gladly tread with them the winepress of anguish and sorrow, and will transmute the bitterest desolation of life's warfare into the sweetest joy, which shall be only the anticipation of the joy to be eternally ours when the God of all consolation shall wipe away all tears from our eyes.[137]

---

[135] 1 Pet. 4:12-13.
[136] Col. 2:11.
[137] Cf. Isa. 25:8; Apoc. 7:17 (RSV = Rev. 7:17).

Chapter Twenty-Two

∾

Give yourself to God

Like every other Jewish mother, Mary submitted to the
law of the purification.[138] She was not bound by the law,
because she was a virgin as well as a mother. But she
obeyed it, hiding her divine motherhood and her miraculous virginity under the mantle of humility. In this mystery, her humility shines forth in all its radiant splendor.
Like Mary, we must never affect singularity, but should
willingly comply with the common usages of society, even
those from which we might justly dispense ourselves.

Great as was her wondrous prerogative, greater still
was the humility that led her to conceal it. Abidingly
conscious of our nothingness, we must realize that God's
favors are not to pander to our pride. Even if our virtue
should exalt us to the spiritual level of him of whom

---

[138]Cf. Lev. 12:2-8.

Christ said, "Amongst those that are born of women, there is not a greater prophet than John the Baptist,"[139] we must never glorify ourselves by courting the admiration and the esteem of others; rather, after the example of our mother, we must use our exaltation to deepen our humility. Holiness is indispensable for us as God's creatures, but let us not forget that the beginning and the end of holiness is humility. The higher the building, the deeper the foundation must be. The spiritual edifice of our sanctity will tower into the heavens only if it is built on the deep, constant conviction of our nothingness. Pride converts the highest virtue into the deadliest vice.

Mary offered her divine Son to the eternal Father and united her own oblation to the offering that Christ made of Himself. With a humility fascinating to the angels, absolute self-extinction vitalizing the sacrifice both of the Child and of His mother, Mary's offering was distinguished by a generosity born of her conscious recognition of her lowliness. An intense yearning to do God's will in all things was its inspiration.

[139] Luke 7:28.

Give yourself to God

In the dedication of herself to the divine will, our Immaculate Mother teaches us our first and most important duty. God has made us for Himself. We belong solely to Him. If we grasped this truth, the wellspring of our spiritual lives would be to glorify God through perfect conformity to His will. Ever appreciating His sovereign dominion over us, we would unhesitatingly make every sacrifice demanded of us and, by the right use of His gifts, return the glory of them to Him who, with infinite liberality, gives them to us for His own greater honor and glory. If we were convinced that we exist not for ourselves, but for God, we would so burn with religious fervor that we would set the souls of our brethren on fire.

The eternal Father gave the most precious treasure that Heaven possessed, His own divine Son, to Mary. In the Temple, Mary returned to the Father His munificent gift by consecrating to His honor and glory her Child, and, for her generosity, the eternal Father made her, through Christ, the dispensatrix of the riches of the Godhead.

Since everything we have is from God, He can recall His gifts from us, their stewards. When He takes back what He has given, it is to make us love Him, the divine Donor, more than His gifts. The supreme and consuming longing to do God's will, which is the same as loving Him above all things, inspired Mary to offer to the eternal Father His and her divine Son. The greatness and grandeur of her reward — her meriting to become with Christ the channel of grace to souls — proves how pleasing to the eternal Father was her detachment when she offered to Him her dearest possession. Let us imitate Mary's generosity, and God will reward us according to the measure of our self-sacrifice in parting with His gifts.

A mother was not obliged by the law of Moses to present and to ransom her firstborn son. In order, however, to free herself from legal uncleanness, she had to submit to the ceremony of purification by presenting herself in the Temple not earlier than the fortieth day after the birth of her first child and by making the offering incumbent upon the poor: two pigeons or turtledoves.

God appraised, not Mary's gift, but the love that inspired it. What we offer to God is valueless in His sight unless the offering is prompted by love. The gift means nothing to Him; the love motivating it means everything. If we love God above all things, we can refuse Him nothing. If we have nothing to offer to Him, we can offer ourselves, and such an oblation will fully compensate for our poverty. No one could have been poorer than Mary, but her love made her gift the richest that was ever offered to God by a creature.

Man considers the external offering. He cannot penetrate beyond it. Man beholds only the face. God looks at the heart. Our self-renunciation is precious in His eyes only when love is at its core.

Chapter Twenty-Three

∽

Allow God to guide your soul

Emphasizing the truth of Mary's rare privileges, the saintly Simeon enlightens her more clearly on the destiny of her divine Child. "Now," he exclaims, "Thou dost dismiss Thy servant, O Lord, according to Thy word, in peace, because my eyes have seen Thy salvation which Thou hast prepared before the face of all peoples: a light to the revelation of the Gentiles and the glory of Thy people Israel."[140]

How many proofs of His paternal love and care did the eternal Father give to the mother of His only-begotten Son! He does the same for the one whom He would lead to the heights of perfection. With divine light, He illumines his mind, thus dispelling his doubts about God's designs upon him, and braces his faith to undergo the

---

[140]Luke 2:29-32.

trials associated with their accomplishment. Mary was too humble to ask of God a grace so great, but He gave it to her at the very moment when and because, in her glorious humility, she least expected it.

Simeon entered the Temple at the moment when the divine Infant was brought in by Mary and Joseph. The holy old man, under the influence of grace, took Christ in his arms and, with the most ardent love, folded Him to his heart. Then, after having gazed on the Expectation of the Nations, the Glory of Israel, and the Redeemer of the World, he asked God to end his earthly sojourn, for he knew that its loftiest moment had been reached.

Mary heard Simeon's words as if they had been spoken to her by God Himself. She meditated on them reverently, kept all of them in her heart, and used them as spiritual food to increase still more her love of God. Indeed, she cherished every word that had been addressed to her about her divine Son. With her soul thrilling to inward bliss and overflowing with the holiest gratitude, the horizon of her knowledge gradually developed in the splendor of divine light. It had begun to shine on her in the house of her cousin Elizabeth, had become more brilliant in her meeting with the shepherds, and was now

approaching its meridian glory in her interview with
Simeon. In each of these notable events of her life, her
confidence in God waxed ever stronger and more secure.

Holy Scripture states very explicitly the frame of mind
of both Mary and Joseph on hearing the prophecy of
Simeon concerning the Savior of men: "And His father
and mother were wondering at those things which were
spoken concerning Him."[141]

The soul over whom God has peculiar designs wonders just as much when it discovers how, through the use
of human agents, He strengthens its faith in the inspirations with which He has blessed it. In a manner that the
soul never dreamed of, God confirms its state, but only
when, corresponding with grace, the soul banishes its
doubts and refrains from vainly prying into His secrets.

The lesson is unmistakable. We must submit wholly
to God, with unwavering faith, serenely confident that
He will give us the necessary light and strength to cooperate with Him in the realization of His designs for us.
The Devil will tempt us to use reason, so prone to error

[141]Luke 2:33.

and illusion, to unravel the mystery of the workings of
the Spirit of God within us. But by flattering our pride,
he will close the eyes of our soul, and because we fail to
conform in artless simplicity to the divine will, we will be
enveloped in the darkness of earth instead of being illumined with the light of Heaven.

Once the will of God is made clear to us, we should
stifle our natural inclinations and patiently wait until God
sees fit to lead us step by step along the path of perfection. Only the soul that humbly does God's bidding —
only the soul that, because of its wholehearted conformity to the divine will, has absolute trust in Him who
feeds the birds of the air — only such a soul will God rid
of anxious fears and gloomy misgivings by gradually pene-
trating it with His divine light. Its full supernatural splendor He will reveal when He shall have accomplished his
designs in the soul.

In so doing, God acts for His own glory and the sanctification of His creatures. How merciful is God in not
unfolding to the soul that He selects for the accomplishment of an extraordinary work, all His designs in the
soul's regard. If such a soul saw at once the full scope of
those designs, with the foreknowledge of the happy issue

of its trials, the soul would lose the reward that God has promised to those who blindly obey Him, and the sacrifices made with the conscious recognition of their happy issue would rob God of the glory that the creature is bound to give the Creator.

Exalted above all other creatures by her eminently unique destiny, Mary never inquired into the manner of its accomplishment. She lived solely by faith. Directed by its heavenly light, she followed it wherever it led her; but such was her self-surrender to God that, had He so willed, she would have been content to remain in darkness.

How divinely eloquent the lesson! Too often, alas, we become dispirited, distressed, or disconsolate when God seems to withdraw from us. The price of our imitation of Mary's abandonment to God is daily self-extinction. We will live wholly to God only when we are wholly dead to ourselves.

Chapter Twenty-Four

Trust in God's promises

The profound and comprehensive prophecy of holy
Simeon reveals a fact of startling significance. It foretells
that Christ, from His advent into the world until the end
of time, shall be a "sign of contradiction,"[142] the occasion
of eternal misery for the wicked and of eternal bliss for
the just, manifesting thereby the secret thoughts of
hearts. What a strange picture of infinite power and
infinite weakness, of supernal glory and worldly igno-
miny, of heavenly light and earthly darkness does Christ
present to mortal eyes! He shall test, and by so doing
shall strengthen, the faith of some, and they will follow
Him. Unbelievers He shall repel, and because of their
unbelief, He shall be the instrument of their everlasting
perdition.

[142]Cf. Luke 2:34.

Mary, to whom Simeon had addressed these words, realized that her Child would be contradicted and utterly rejected by the Jews who had, for forty centuries, unceasingly sighed for Him, their Savior. She also understood that history would repeat itself. She knew that myriads even of His faithful followers throughout the world would turn from Him and through their bitter hostility to His teaching, both by word and by example, by setting man's fallible opinion before God's infallible word, by open and daringly profligate conduct, by fear of the world's judgment and expectation of worldly advantage, would make His coming the occasion of their eternal ruin.

Simeon also convinced Mary that she would share in the suffering and sorrow of her divine Son. "And thy own soul," he said, "a sword shall pierce."[143] How clear and explicit these words are! The sword that will pierce Christ's body will transfix Mary's soul. Her Child, by becoming the King of Martyrs, will make her their queen. Her sorrow will be as great as the sea.

This ominous prophecy of future trial did not disturb Mary's peace of mind, because her will was one with the

---

[143]Luke 2:35.

will of God. This it was that begot in her sensitive soul perfect union with the sufferings of her Child.

What a marked disparity between the woeful prediction of Simeon and the joyous tidings of the archangel Gabriel announcing the unutterable greatness, the unimaginable glory, of the Redeemer of men! Mary undoubtedly noted the seeming contradiction; but, pondering in her heart every word addressed to her about her divine Son, she knew, with her lively faith, that God, who reveals His plans only gradually to His creatures, would in due time reconcile it.

And here Mary teaches us a very fundamental lesson. In order to live, not to ourselves, but to God, we must bear the Cross in union with Christ. Mary was the Queen of Martyrs because she was most intimately united with the King of Martyrs. She suffered with Christ, experiencing in her soul what He underwent in His body. The union of their suffering was perfect.

If we are to imitate our Mother, we must never separate our sufferings from the sufferings of Christ. This bond of sympathy between us and our crucified God will sustain us no matter how heavy our cross. Indeed, we will suffer with joy if we realize that Christ is suffering with us and in us, that He sends us the cross only so that He may trace His image in our souls by uniting us more closely with Him.

Bearing the cross in union with Christ, we will carry it, not faintheartedly, not fretfully, but like Mary, with tranquillity, lovingly resigned to His will. And the fore-knowledge of suffering will not depress us or make us recoil through the consciousness of our own frailty. Firmly believing that God will support us in the hour of trial, we will not undermine our spiritual strength by fruitlessly anticipating that hour but, with true Christian courage, will patiently await help from on high, implicitly confident that God will give it at the opportune moment and according to the measure of our need of it.

But to mount to the highest spiritual level, we must do more than suffer in union with Christ. To possess the spirit of suffering fully, we must neither curiously investigate the designs of Divine Providence nor try to harmonize the manifestation at one period with the apparently contradictory revelation of God's will at a later period. In not disclosing to us His plans all at once, in seeming to contradict Himself by His revelations, God wishes us to store up great merit. Mary did not strive to square the words of the archangel Gabriel with those of holy Simeon. Her faith taught her that the predictions of both were inspired by the Holy Spirit, and she left it to God to reconcile their apparent inconsistency. Let us imitate our Mother in this respect, and God, in His infinite wisdom, will make all things work together unto our good.

Chapter Twenty-Five

Seek glory for God alone

Despite the sacrifices entailed, the Magi, enlightened by
God, corresponded with His grace decisively, perseveringly, and with absolute confidence.

The recognition and adoration of her divine Son by
the Magi was a source of great consolation to Mary. He
who had become man to die for all men was first seen
and adored by the Jews, represented by the shepherds,
and afterward by the Gentiles, in the persons of the
Magi.

Interiorly illumined by grace and exteriorly guided
by the striking appearance of a star in the East, they left
home and country and, directed by "the magnificent language of Heaven," journeyed to Judea in quest of Christ.
They inquired of Herod about the birthplace of the newborn King: "Where is He that is born King of the Jews?
For we have seen His star in the East and are come to

adore Him."[144] The scribes and Pharisees told them of the prophecy that Christ would be born in Bethlehem. As they resumed their journey, the star that had disappeared on their entrance into Jerusalem reappeared in all its heavenly splendor; and, "seeing the star, they rejoiced with exceeding great joy. It went before them until it came and stood over where the Child was. And entering into the house, they found the Child with Mary, His mother. And falling down, they adored Him. And opening their treasures, they offered Him gifts: gold, frankincense, and myrrh."[145]

We can imagine these three rulers, overcome by supernatural joy, narrating to Mary, with beautiful simplicity, their personal history and captivating her with their eloquent account of the mysterious star that had led them to Christ. Having adored their God, they indubitably paid their reverent regards to her, His mother. But their tribute of veneration did not awaken within her the slightest feeling of pride. It made her only all the more humble. Her love of God was such that she referred their kingly

[144]Matt. 2:2.
[145]Matt. 2:10-11.

homage to Christ, with whom she was one in the redemption of souls. The dominant thought of Mary's mind,
the overpowering sentiment of her soul while they were
greeting her with cordial reverence, was one of profound
gratitude to God for having revealed His divine Son to
the pagan nations of the world, thus aiding them to free
themselves from the slavery of idolatry.

How can we describe her happiness when she witnessed the adoration of her Child by these learned kings,
who would with burning enthusiasm teach their subjects,
both by word and example, the wonders of divine love
that emanated from the crib of the infant Savior? Her joy,
however, was not selfish. She rejoiced in virtue of the
honor, love, and adoration that the regal Magi, from
the depths of their souls, lavished upon her divine Son.
The greatest simplicity had characterized Mary's interview with the shepherds. Enchanting humility was its
distinctive charm during the visit of the Magi. Their adoration of Christ and their respectful homage to her only
intensified her unselfish love of her God.

Any unusual consideration, especially from the powerful ones of earth, tends to feed the pride that is so intimately interwoven with weak human nature. But far

from contributing to Mary's self-complacency, the tribute of veneration paid to her by the three kings only subserved her self-effacement by increasing her humility.

The will of God being the ruling power of her life, she beheld, with the eyes of pure faith, the working of grace in their souls. It was grace that moved them to come from afar. God had called them, and they obeyed His call. It was grace that strengthened them to overcome the perils of their long, difficult, and wearisome journey. It was grace that nerved them to inquire fearlessly concerning the birth of Christ. It was grace that made them beard the lion in his den, for they doubtless knew who Herod was, how insanely jealous of those claiming equality with him. It was grace that made them recognize Christ as King of Heaven and earth. It was grace that drew from them their tribute of homage to the Mother of the Redeemer.

Recognizing the operation of grace in their souls, Mary, far from hindering its supernatural action, allowed them freely to express their sentiments of love and joy. Spiritually delighted with their gratitude to God, she valued their veneration just insofar as it tended to His glory.

Only a great soul, only a soul most closely united with God, can relinquish the glory given to it by returning it wholly to God.

If we are to forego ourselves entirely and make the honor and the distinction flowing from God's gifts redound, not to our own glory, but to that of our best Benefactor, humility like Mary's is essential. It may be categorically stated that her fathomless humility convinced the Magi that she was the Mother of God, for who but the Mother of God could be exalted above men and angels and still be nothing in her own eyes?

Chapter Twenty-Six

Rely on God's Providence

The fear of losing his crown, born of the wild passion of jealousy, so wrought upon the corrupt mind and depraved heart of the ruthless Herod that he resolved to kill his infant rival. But just as it might have seemed that his brutal scheme would succeed, "behold an angel of the Lord appeared in sleep to Joseph, saying, 'Arise, and take the Child and His mother, and fly into Egypt; and be there until I shall tell thee. For it will come to pass that Herod will seek the Child to destroy Him.' Who arose and took the Child and His mother by night and retired into Egypt. And he was there until the death of Herod."[146]

Not to Mary, but to Joseph, did the angel manifest God's will. But such was Mary's self-effacement that she did not debate with herself why God showed His

[146]Matt. 2:13-14.

preference for her chaste spouse. From the mere view-point of reason, it would seem that God should have honored her rather than Joseph, because she was the mother of the divine Child and Joseph was only His foster father. She was assuredly as solicitous as Joseph about protecting the life of her Son. Had God spoken to her through His angel, or to her and Joseph simultaneously, she would have felt greater confidence. Had Mary been the slave of self-love, thoughts like these would naturally have crossed her mind.

By the self-extinction that she exhibited instead, she teaches us to receive and execute God's will even though He speaks to us by those who are perhaps our inferiors in virtue, and thus to conquer the insinuating and subtle passion of pride.

Incomprehensibly exalted above Joseph because of the divine maternity, Mary, in her great humility, considered Joseph, as head of the Holy Family, better fitted to receive the message of Heaven than she, the mother of the divine Child. We must try to practice this lesson taught so persuasively by her whom God raised to the pinnacle of greatness. "Let every soul," says St. Paul, "be subject to higher powers. For there is no power but from God; and those that are, are ordained of God."[147] God reveals His will through the channels of ecclesiastical or civil authority. And strange as it may seem, we should actually rely more on this indirect communication than if He apparently spoke to us directly, because the Devil, "a liar, and the father thereof," is ever ready to deceive us by pretended revelations, since "truth is not in him."[148] Moreover, we are morally certain of God's will in our regard only when the judgment of our spiritual director concurs with the voice of conscience. "He who tries to direct himself," exclaims St. Bernard, "makes himself the disciple of a fool."

Mary's faith was severely tried by the command of the angel to flee into Egypt. Her Son was the Son of the Most High; yet she, His mother, must defend Him, the King of kings, from the vengeance of an earthly sovereign by flight into a pagan land. Her Child was the God of infinite power. Could He not, then, remain in Bethlehem and crush with a mere word the tyrant who sought His life? Why must the infinite God flee from His finite creature?

[147]Rom. 13:1.
[148]John 8:44.

Why must He subject Himself, by a precipitate flight, to the dangers of a sojourn in a heathen country? Mary must have been severely tried by such thoughts. Humanly speaking, the glowing prophecy of Gabriel that of Christ's kingdom there would be no end seemed completely set at naught by the present plight of its King.

Then, too, Mary and Joseph were without resources and knew nothing about the land to which they were to direct their steps, except that it was pagan. What could they expect there but persecution? As a believer in the one true God, Joseph would find it hard to ply his trade successfully for their support among idolaters. Nor did they know how long their painful banishment would last. It required more than human courage to encounter and to conquer obstacles so great.

But despite the severity of the trial, Mary's mind was at rest. Her afflicted maternal feelings were not prejudicial to her total abandonment to God's will. Without voluntary anxiety and fear, she obeyed immediately and started in the darkness of the night on her long journey with her divine Child and Joseph. She had nothing to fear for herself, for Joseph, or for her Son, because she carried her God in her arms.

~

No matter how heavy our cross, provided Christ is with us through our full submission to His will, we shall, like Mary, clothed with the strength of God, face calmly even the fury of Hell.

The conduct of Mary and Joseph on learning the will of God is worthy of our absorbing study and our whole-hearted imitation. They did not allege as an excuse for not obeying the command of Heaven the difficulties of the journey or its dangers to them and their divine treasure. They were neither tossed to and fro in a tumult of doubt and indecision, nor did they attempt their hard task with the certainty of failing. Theirs was religion in the finest sense of the word: blind obedience to God.

Their stay in a pagan land must have been very unpleasant; but they awaited a definite sign from Heaven before returning to Galilee.

Once we surrender ourselves to the divine will, obedience must be our solace and support. We must disregard the doubts with which Satan inspires us, by acting against them in confidence that God will provide for us even though to do so might cost Him a miracle. Absolutely secure through the practice of loving obedience, we will distrust our own judgment, and no unchristian anxiety for tomorrow will disturb us while we are busied in present services. Lowly obedience will keep our minds joyously free from vague fears and uncertain, indefinite surmises about the future. We will view God in His tranquil Providence with the assurance that He will always take into account our eternal interests. Thus only through complete conformity to His will can we ensure our own peacefulness of soul and promote the glory of our Creator.

∽

Chapter Twenty-Seven

Approach the eucharistic Christ for enlightenment

Words cannot describe the sorrow of Mary's maternal heart when she realized the melancholy fact that she had lost her Child, her God. Yet it was with an entire absence of tumult and feverish emotion, with a love calm, full, reverent, and contemplative, and a mind disciplined into submission to God, that she and the silently sorrowful Joseph sought Him among their kinsfolk and acquaintances.

As He withdrew from Mary and Joseph, so Jesus often withdraws unexpectedly from souls serving Him with all possible fervor. Then sorrow rives their hearts. In the anguish of their desolation — for what loss can be compared to the loss of God? — they sift their consciences and, with meticulous introspection, examine and grieve over their smallest faults.

But their fears are groundless. Christ has not abandoned them. He hides Himself from them to prove the sincerity of their love of Him, to divest it of selfishness and impart to it a truer tone and character. They will gain spiritual light, as did Mary, at the price of serene surrender of themselves to the unseen God — not by bewailing the loss of sensible devotion, but by silently grieving over the apparent privation of their God. In their distress of soul, they will, like Mary, glorify Him by making the agony of their loss bind them to Him more closely than ever.

And they must imitate the Blessed Mother in their quest of Him. With love kindled to undying ardor, she sought Him everywhere. How pleasing to her God was her practical maternal solicitude! If, sensing the greatness of our loss, we seek Christ as Mary did, we will be all the more keenly and lovingly conscious of the joy of His presence when we find Him.

Wondrously inventive are the ways of divine love. If we always felt the delights of Christ's presence within us, we would (for such is the force of habit) fail to appraise so inestimable a gift at its true value. Whereas if, bereft of sensible fervor and desolate with sorrow, we love God above all things, perceiving our great need of Him, we will redouble our efforts to recover our lost treasure. We will pray better, be more recollected, be more indifferent to the life that is so empty without God, and be intent on one thing only: His immediate return.

We need not travel far. We will not find Him among worldlings, who cast down moral excellence from its true position and enthrone in its place the usurping empire of mere reason, who are so elated over the findings of science, conversant as it is with experiments on material creation, as to treat God with scorn or to forget His existence. Nor will we discover Him among our kinsfolk and acquaintances.

Like Mary, we will find Him in His temple, in His house. There He dwells day and night, anxiously awaiting our arrival. There we will discern His presence, but only with the eyes of faith.

When we stagger under the protracted pressure of temptation and are benumbed by the bleaching winds of spiritual aridity, let us approach the fire ever burning in the tabernacle. "In a desert land, and where there is no way and no water: so in the sanctuary have I come before

Thee, to see Thy power and Thy glory."[149] Yes, we will see His veiled glory and be strengthened with His power if we visit Him in His temple and tell Him what affrights us, what burdens us.

The divine silence of Christ in His school of love, the tabernacle, will breathe into our souls the peace of God and will make our burdens light. In the presence of the eucharistic King, we will learn every phase of the science of salvation. There we will acquire from the source of all wisdom what books cannot impart unless they stress the knowledge of Christ, the knowledge alone necessary.

Illumined by the light emanating from the tabernacle, we can cultivate a graciously reverent familiarity with Christ, a privilege unknown to fear and cold respect, a privilege issuing solely from pure love for our Lord and Master. Like Mary, who said to her Child, "Son, why hast Thou done so to us? Behold, Thy father and I have sought Thee sorrowing,"[150] we can, with devotional freedom, ask the God of the Eucharist to enlighten us about

[149]Ps. 62:3 (RSV = Ps. 63:1-2).
[150]Luke 2:48.

His Providence in our regard. We can exchange confidences, much to the delight of our infinite Lover.

God does not stand on ceremony with His children. He does not exact of them trembling fear and dread circumspection. He desires them to come to Him with humble simplicity and to talk with Him with childlike candor, telling Him in the language of the heart, rather than the measured accents of the tongue, of the pain that His crosses inflict and the grief that saddens their souls. But they alone who, like Mary, do God's will perfectly can speak to Christ with such childlike familiarity.

In answering His mother's question, Christ emphasized His divinity: "How is it that you sought me? Did you not know that I must be about my Father's business?"[151] It was her maternal love that prompted Mary's interrogation. The Savior of men would, by His reply, have her rise above the natural and focus her vision first and foremost on His divinity, veiled from mortal eyes by His human nature. The very tone of His voice and the majesty of His manner could not but prove to Mary and Joseph, as well as to the doctors of the Law, that He was God as well as

[151]Luke 2:49.

man. Being God and therefore one with His heavenly Father, He put the interests of that Father above His own. From the tenor of His answer to Mary, it is evident that He also desired to teach her detachment and so to prepare her for her final separation from Him at the foot of the Cross.

Holy Scripture remarks, "And they understood not the word that He spoke unto them,"[152] thus proving that it was a part of the divine plan to unfold only gradually even to Mary and Joseph the great work the divine Christ had come on earth to accomplish. Deaf to the suggestions of her natural maternal love, the Virgin Mother did not inquire into the hidden meaning of Christ's words.

How heroic her self-renunciation! What a lesson parents may learn from her example! She loved God above all things. Thus she generously sacrificed the ties of flesh and blood which are, alas, too often an obstacle in doing God's will.

Herein Mary teaches most clearly the duty of parents concerning the vocation of their child. They may examine the nature of his calling, but they must not frustrate,

[152]Luke 2:50.

for any reason whatsoever, the will of God in his regard. The Author of nature, since He has dowered the heart of man with human affections, would not have His grace destroy them. Rather, He would have it restrain them when they become inordinate, and so subject them to His love. After the example of Jesus and Mary, both parents and children must make their Father's business the paramount issue of their lives. This they will do only when they submit with loving docility, and regardless of the sacrifice, to the recognized will of God.

Chapter Twenty-Eight

∞

Practice humility in commanding and in obeying

Obedience epitomized the life of Christ: "He went
down with them and came to Nazareth and was subject
to them";[153] "He humbled Himself, becoming obedient
unto death, even to the death of the Cross."[154] Without
obedience, our religious ideas lie on the mere surface of
our mind and have no root within it. The chief charm of
the hidden life of Christ was His lowly subjection. It was
His practice of the difficult virtue of obedience that gave
to the holy obscurity of Nazareth its sweetness, its tranquillity, and its majesty.

Let us rest awhile in the humble dwelling of Jesus,
Mary, and Joseph. There we will learn the science of

[153] Luke 2:51.
[154] Phil. 2:8.

right living. There we will acquire the free, unconstrained spirit of true devotion by studying the virtues that made the home of the Holy Family a veritable paradise.

How staggering the thought that the Son of God was for thirty years subject to His creatures Mary and Joseph! And consider their poverty. They were satisfied with only the necessities of life and very often were without even those. But with their minds centered on God, they enjoyed His benefactions from the common store of nature's bounty. They did not seek help from their neighbors. They did not rove after the goods of the world. They indulged no visions of "the earth and the fullness thereof,"[155] because their hearts were permanently attached to higher things; God was the point of rest for their minds' eye. They lived in retirement and were familiar only with God.

It never dawned on the people of Nazareth that the Son of God and His Virgin Mother dwelt among them. While they were doubtless edified by the conduct of the Holy Family, they did not know of the divine dignity of

[155]Ps. 23:1 (RSV = Ps. 24:1).

Christ and the miraculous prerogatives of Mary. Neither the mother nor the reputed father of the divine Child anticipated the designs of Heaven. They waited patiently until it pleased God to reveal to the expectant world the astounding mystery of the Incarnation.

With their minds composed, their wishes subdued, and their tempers ever heavenly, profound peace reigned in the hearts of Mary and Joseph. Divine love united them. Grace poured constantly from its source — Christ — into the soul of His mother, and she was the channel through which it was imparted to His foster father. What unceasing interchange of holy thought between Christ and Mary and between her and her saintly spouse! Christ was the object of the uninterrupted, enthralling contemplation of both. We cannot, therefore, measure their growth in holiness. It was a source of light, freedom, and consolation to them to have Him ever before them.

We can well imagine the character of their conversation in the presence of their God. With what eloquence beyond the power of words they must have thanked Him for His mercy to fallen man! While their hands were busy, He absorbed their thoughts and affections and thrilled their hearts with the purest love for Him. He, their Child, was ever speaking to their souls. What food for thought was His obedience to them! How they treasured the words that fell from His divine lips!

But although interiorly they adored their God, exteriorly they did His will by the discreet exercise of their authority over Him. And He, their God, obeyed them. Their commands were distinguished by considerateness, by a most charming humility, and by a habitual sense of their immeasurable inferiority to Him, together with a love springing from their ardent admiration of His subjection to them who were but dust and ashes.

What glory Christ gave to His eternal Father by thus annihilating Himself before His creatures through His loving obedience to them! We cannot comprehend this subjection. Nor can we understand the self-extinction wrought by grace in their souls that enabled them to command their divine Child in full accord with His will.

How admirable is Mary because of the virtues that she thus practiced as she imposed her wishes on her divine Son in obedience to His own desire. Every command increased her humility and thus, by complete death of self, contributed to the greater glory of God. She was wholly under the dominion of grace; God's glory and her own total self-effacement were the twin sentiments of her heart and soul.

Obedience to lawful authority is often against the current of human feeling and opinion and the course of the world. But the end of living, according to the world's wisdom, is utter estrangement from God — moral ruin. Are we bound by the yoke of the world's bondage, by its inordinate pride and its overbearing self-sufficiency? If self-will is our lord and master, we are not Christ's, for "they that are Christ's have crucified their flesh, with the vices and concupiscences."[156] We cannot die to ourselves, unless we obey. What a stimulus to obedience is the absorbing contemplation of the spectacle of the eternal God debasing Himself to the dust by full submission to His creatures: "He was subject to them."

Impressive beyond words is the lesson of our Lord's obedience. Equally impressive is the lesson of Mary's exercise of her authority. A ruler, whether ecclesiastical or civil, has not inherent but only delegated rights over his subjects. If he realizes this truth, he will command with

[156]Gal. 5:24.

charity, with meekness, with humility, and with due deference to the feelings of those over whom he has been placed. Let him but convince himself that he is responsible to God for the use of his authority, and he will command like Him whom he represents. Only he who has learned to obey can rule. But for either commanding or obeying, humility is indispensable. A ruler without humility is a tyrant. A subject without humility is an anarchist.

Chapter Twenty-Nine

Seek holiness through your daily work

Great is the power and fascination of the life of Mary at
Nazareth. It was a life of obscurity, contemplation, and
labor. Singularity and distinction found no place in this
school of eminent virtue. The ordinary engaged Mary's
love and devotion. Although Heaven had honored her
with revelations and miracles beyond understanding, she
gave herself heart and soul with graceful ease to the commonplace. An enchanting simplicity beautified the performance of each of her domestic duties. Her whole day's
work was done for God alone, because prayer, simple and
sublime, permeated it. The ardor of her piety ran its course
daily without ever attracting attention. The self-conceit
of human nature, which would in others naturally flow
from the consciousness of exaltation, never darkened
Mary's mind, because the thought of God absorbed her.

Accordingly, her disposition was serene and her manner majestic in its unearthly calmness.

Without fidelity to the commonplace, our chief religious duties will lack stability and perseverance. We should live in such a way that God, who "searcheth the reins and the hearts,"[157] may be able to regard us with pleasure. Mere externals are worthless in God's sight. He looks within. We must edify our neighbor, but to do so, our conduct need in no way be remarkable.

In imitation of Mary, our lives must be hidden and obscure. She never sought the circles of the elite. Her heart was in her home, and hence she could not be carried on with the stream of the world. She took no interest in the world's multitude of matters, because she was ever alive to the reality of things unseen. Only through charity or necessity did she leave the precincts of her holy dwelling. She had a deep supernatural sense of the fitness of things. She did not, then, court the company of what the world considers superior society. Indeed, she mingled only seldom, even with the lowly inhabitants of Nazareth.

---

[157] Apoc. 2:23 (RSV = Rev. 2:23).

Grace and courtesy inspired her visits. They were noted for their charity. She eschewed gossip. She was not voluble, because she always strove to edify her neighbor by her conversation. Although the Mother of God, she wished to pass as the most insignificant of His creatures. What a rebuke to the pride that thrives on God's gifts and yearns to live in their reflected glory! Her hidden sanctity was carefully concealed beneath the noiseless tenor of her daily life.

To copy Mary's example in this particular respect requires virtue of no ordinary kind. The utmost care, through constant fidelity to grace, is necessary to hide such workings of the presence of God within us. Self-love, our worst enemy, will ever suggest display or betray us into some indiscretion that usually tends to sever our union with our Creator.

But we are not to suppose that the life of Mary at Nazareth was inactive because it was wholly given to prayer. To entertain such a notion would be to misunderstand the meaning of prayer entirely. Prayer is not mere passive contemplation. It is action. Mary was not the victim of indolent self-indulgence. She was too poor to be inactive. Her poverty made work a necessity. But both her labor

in discharging faithfully the duties of her domestic life
and whatever leisure she had were dedicated to uninterrupted communion with the God whose presence she
never forgot.

If we are to grow in holiness, we must labor. We cannot lead interior lives without labor. In times of spiritual
dryness, moreover, work will divert our attention from
the difficulties necessarily associated with aridity. The
Devil is most successful with idlers. He wastes no time
on those who are busily engaged. Without work, we will
enjoy inordinately the delights of sensible devotion and
thus mistake an accident of sanctity for its substance.
Without work, sanctity, in all its comprehensive unity,
is impossible.

Mary's holiness kept pace with her labor. Through her
faithful performance of her ordinary duties, she may be
said to have attained, in the solitude of Nazareth, her
greatest sanctity.

Our piety is so superficial that we are apt to value
such a life as meaningless in the acquisition of virtue.
Even in things spiritual, the marvelous and the brilliant
affect us most. We are deeply impressed by rigid fasts and
by prolific prayer. So weak is human nature that the

uncommon inevitably serves to increase our pride. The Pharisees were bent on doing the extraordinary. They prayed long and fasted much. It was the pride behind all this that made Christ reject them.

But as the generality of men are created to do, not the extraordinary, but the ordinary, we must, after the example of Mary, appraise a life of obscurity, constant labor, and daily fidelity to the commonplace as the surest stepping-stone to sainthood.

How many saints there are in Heaven who on earth did only the ordinary!

Chapter Thirty

∾

Pattern your life on Christ's

Christ became man not only to die for us, but also to teach us how to live, to be our example. The practical imitation of Christ is our supreme achievement. We can best learn to imitate Him from His mirror — Mary, our mother — who reflects His spirit most powerfully and most faithfully.

The imitation of her divine Son was the great occupation of Mary's life. It thrilled her with the purest joy to have so perfect a Model ever before her, to talk freely and often with Him, and to be so close an observer of His conduct. Being of one mind with Him, since she was His mother, she realized that she must imitate Him perfectly. She therefore fed her mind solely and unceasingly with His perfections. She meditated on all His words and recorded them in her heart. The acquisition of His spirit absorbed her. She spent herself and was spent in learning the practical knowledge of Jesus Christ. Mary gave herself to the assiduous study of His virtues, not curiously, as men pore over science, but with a view to perfect imitation of Him, her God. In so doing, she became the holiest creature that ever adorned the earth — a Vessel of Singular Devotion[158] indeed.

If we are to be children worthy of such a mother, we must burn with the desire to imitate our Lord and Master. Let us pursue our study earnestly and perseveringly, as Mary did, and thus gain the practical knowledge that will be for us eternal life; for "this is eternal life, that they may know Thee, the only true God, and Jesus Christ, whom Thou hast sent."[159] No matter what our vocation, whether we are rich or poor, healthy or sick, socially prominent or buried in obscurity, whether we are consecrated to God in the religious state or live in the world, we cannot be true Christians unless we daily strive to resemble Christ. The more we study His life, the more fascinating it will become; the more we seek to exhaust

[158]One of the titles given to Mary in the Litany of the Blessed Mother.
[159]John 17:3.

it, the more we will find its content inexhaustible. The usages and the persuasions of interest must not deter us from this study, indispensable for salvation. All other knowledge to the exclusion of this may throne us in the power of the world, but only to annul our heavenly election.

Mary did not have to give up the kind of engrossing pursuit that indisposes the mind to the knowledge and imitation of Christ. The study of His words and actions, both during His mortal career and after His death, was the chief duty of her life. She was a total stranger to the rank, station, intelligence, and riches of worldlings. She had none of the world's accomplishments. She was without worldly wisdom. But none ever surpassed, none ever equaled her in the knowledge that alone is necessary. None knew Christ as Mary knew Him.

We grossly misunderstand the meaning of *sanctity* if we content ourselves with a mere fitful study of our perfect Model. No writer has ever done justice to the life of Christ. Its eloquence, its instructiveness, its depth, and its comprehensiveness are beyond the grasp of the human mind. The doctrine of Christ is not and never will be fully developed. His example has never been, nor ever

will be, fully reduced to practice. If we study His doctrine
and example superficially, we waste time, insult the God
who commands us to walk in the footsteps of His divine
Son, and retard our progress on the heavenward road.
We must first convince ourselves of the necessity of the
knowledge of Christ's doctrine and example, and then no
sacrifice will be too great to possess this divine science.
We must read His life with both head and heart. We must
peruse authors who are filled with His spirit. We must
study Christ dwelling within us and ever speaking to
our souls.

Not to vaunt our vanity, but to further our own spiritual progress and to help along the highways of holiness
those under our care should be the motives of the most
absorbing and most fascinating of all studies, the engrossing theme of our Lord and Master.

Our study of Christ must be, above all things, practical. It must bear upon our conduct. A mere speculative
knowledge of Him will conduce to the service of God
only insofar as His service does not interfere with the
service of the world.

As our intelligence is very feeble in all inquiries
into moral and religious truth, we must focus on this

delightful study, not the dim, uncertain light of reason, but the light of Heaven, the constant concomitant of grace. If our imitation of Christ is proportioned to our knowledge of Him, we shall receive greater graces in order to know Him better and follow Him more closely. To use grace and the lights that accompany it only to foster barren speculation on the life of Christ will quench in us all desire to imitate Him, because the imitation of Christ is the direct result of corresponding with grace and walking in its heavenly illumination. The intensity of our soul's desire to follow in the footsteps of our Master is measured by our actual imitation of Him.

We must be as reasonable in spiritual matters as in temporal. The professed inquirer after natural truths always tries to exhaust their meaning. We must not be less rational in our endeavors to know Christ. We must study the inward character of His life. We must read His heart. To do this, we must live in His heart. There and there only will we discover the hidden springs of His teachings, the fountainhead of His example.

And if we are free from sin and yearn to imitate her divine Son, Mary, the Queen of Saints, will enshrine us in His heart, because she is His most perfect imitator.

Chapter Thirty-One

∽

Pray with humility and perseverance

What a free, unconstrained spirit of joy must have animated the guests at the marriage feast of Cana in Galilee in virtue of the presence of Jesus and Mary! Indeed, we cannot truly rejoice without Jesus and Mary. They are the source of all joy, natural and supernatural. As they did for the newly married couple, our Lord and His mother will safeguard with their presence the joy of our social festivities against confusion, embarrassment, and sin.

"And the wine failing, the Mother of Jesus saith to Him, 'They have no wine.' "[160] How lovingly considerate is Mary's implied request! As if to prove the greatness of her love for souls, she asks her Son to perform a miracle for the distressed bride and groom. It was Christ, the God of love, who inspired her petition. He did not have to be

---

[160] John 2:3.

told that the wine had failed, because, as God, He was omniscient. From eternity, He foreknew that He would work the first miracle of His public life at the behest of His mother. We must grasp these facts if we wish to understand Christ's answer.

"And Jesus saith to her, 'Woman, what is that to me and to thee? My hour is not yet come.' "[161] Those who see in Christ's words a rebuke to His Virgin Mother utterly fail to penetrate their deep, hidden meaning. It is unthinkable that He would repulse His mother when she asked Him, her Son and her God, to do an act of charity for souls in distress. Why should He hurt her feelings when He had already determined to obey her? The fact that He worked the miracle shows that He was pleased with her discreet request.

Christ wished, by His reply to Mary, which was consonant with His divine dignity and most respectful to her, to demonstrate to His hearers that He was God as well as man. Far from being disrespectful, the term *woman*, in the sense in which our Lord used it, was one of reverence and love; in Hebrew, the term means "lady." Mary's direction

[161]John 2:4.

to the waiters, "Whatsoever He shall say to you, do ye,"[162] proves beyond all doubt that she regarded her Son's answer as a striking manifestation of His special love for her.

It is indeed of rare significance that Christ, in strengthening the faith of His disciples by His obedience to His mother, made the revelation of His divinity the effect of her intercession. When our Lord changed the water to wine, He did not pay a debt to Mary as man, since, as man, He could not perform miracles; He did her bidding as God, through His infinite compassion. The miracle was wholly gratuitous. Nevertheless, what a clear manifestation it was of the mind of Christ in regard to His mother! In His kingdom, she is to be the almoner of the King's largess.

Again, Christ wished to teach, by His answer to Mary, that He became man to do, not His own will, but the will of His Father. His whole life had been divinely planned. He would act only in obedience to the divine decrees. He would not perform miracles to reveal His power or to satisfy the curiosity of His followers; He would work them

---

[162] John 2:5.

only at the time ordained by His Father and to reward strong, living faith, like Mary's.

Above all, He was eager, before obeying His mother, to test her faith and humility. And they stood the test, because Christ changed the water into wine. What a significant lesson Mary teaches us by this unlimited confidence in the power and goodness of her divine Son! Illumined by God, she knew that Christ would grant her request. She therefore said to the waiters, "Whatsoever He shall say to you, do ye." She might have said, "All things are possible to him that believeth."[163]

This first known miracle of His public career is a magnificent commentary on Mary's power with Christ. From her conduct we should learn never to oppose the divine will, even though conformity to it may mean a very severe trial of our faith, or even our profound humiliation. The prayer of lively and persevering faith God will always answer; yes, He will work miracles for such a prayer. "Truly I say to you, if you have faith as a grain of mustard seed, you will say to this mountain, 'Move from here to there,'

[163]Mark 9:22.

and it will move; and nothing will be impossible to you."[164] The eye of the soul of the suppliant who prays thus is sound, because the greater glory of God and the sanctification of his soul are his chief concern. God has inspired his prayer; He must therefore answer it, since He ever works for His own greater glory and the spiritual welfare of His creatures.

With the Apostles, we should ask Christ to teach us how to pray. After the example of Mary, our petition should be persevering and pervaded by a deep sense of our own nothingness. It will then touch our Lord's heart, and even if He apparently refuses to hear us, our insistence and our humility will infallibly move Him to pity, and He will answer our prayer.

---

[164]Matt. 17:19 (RSV translation).

Chapter Thirty-Two

Conform your will to God's will

The life of Mary, like her divine Son's, was a daily crucifixion and martyrdom. She found the Cross very heavy
during the three years of His public life, for then Christ
had to leave her side so that He might be "about His
Father's business,"[165] the sanctification and salvation of
souls. But although deprived of the joy of His sensible
presence, she was more intimately united with Him than
ever through her sacrificial love wrought by conformity
to His will. By estranging Himself from her, Christ was
preparing His mother for her final separation from Him
at the foot of the Cross.

Very likely, nonetheless, with the other holy women,
she followed Him up and down Galilee. In these jour-
neys, Mary was dependent upon her saintly companions

[165]Luke 2:49.

for her livelihood, because St. Joseph had been called
to his eternal reward. Free from her domestic duties, she
could now give all her time to her Son. But while she
yearned with the full ardor of her saintly soul to devote
herself exclusively to Him, He, so to speak, abandoned
her entirely. The evangelists mention no word uttered by
Christ to His Mother from the time of His first miracle
until just before He expired on the Cross. More than
once, He seemed not even to recognize her.

"As He was yet speaking to the multitudes," says St.
Matthew, "behold, His mother and His brethren stood
without, seeking to speak to Him. And one said to Him,
'Behold, Thy mother and Thy brethren stand without,
seeking Thee.' But He, answering him that told Him,
said, 'Who is my mother, and who are my brethren?'
And stretching forth His hand toward His disciples, He
said, 'Behold my mother and my brethren. For whosoever
shall do the will of my Father that is in Heaven, he is my
brother, and sister, and mother.' "[166] With these significant words, Christ taught the multitude that, publicly,
when He was intent only on His Father's business, He

[166]Matt. 12:46-50.

196

recognized not a blood relationship, but a spiritual one. He emphasized the truth that they alone who do the will of His Father are His brethren, His sisters, and His mother. This is the only tie that He countenances.

Thus did Christ declare to the Jews His divinity by announcing unequivocally to them that His sole mission on earth was to make known to men the will of His Father and to instruct them how to do it. In full logical consonance with this, He appraised spiritual relationships as unimaginably higher than the ties of flesh and blood. And the basis of a spiritual relationship is complete conformity to the will of His Father, in imitation of Him who always did the things that pleased the Father.

What eloquent praise are Christ's words on the life of Mary! Transcendent as was her dignity as Mother of God according to the flesh, her spiritual motherhood was incomparably more astonishing and endeared her immeasurably more to her divine Son. We will never appreciate Mary's supereminent sanctity unless we understand the intimacy of her union with Christ in virtue of her spiritual maternity. "The Virgin is pronounced blessed," says St. Augustine, "because she did the will of the Father. This it was that our Lord extolled in her."

The School of Mary

∽

We cannot imitate our mother if we fail to participate in her most exalted dignity. But every Christian can share her spiritual motherhood, provided he pays the price for this rare privilege. We must, like her, surrender ourselves irrevocably to Christ; we must never shrink from suffering. The Cross is the measure of God's love for us and the sum total of our love for God. Only when we have understood Mary's martyrdom will we comprehend the greatness of Christ's love for His mother and the intensity of her love for her Son. To be willing, like Mary, to relinquish the delights of sensible devotion and the happiness of Christ's heavenly communications, to submit heart and soul to His apparent withdrawal from us — when we have learned to do this, then and only then can we share in Mary's spiritual motherhood.

To do the will of God: this was the Blessed Virgin's keenest joy. Here is the truth we must grasp before we can imitate her. It was Mary's exclusive privilege to be Christ's mother according to the flesh. Not for this reason, however, was she the object of His particular love. Her progress in virtue, her humility, her detachment from earth's unsatisfactory gifts, her willingness to suffer, her interior joy in bearing the Cross — in short, her imitation of Christ through resignation to His will — constituted her moral worth with God, and to this source alone can we trace Christ's special love for her.

Our sanctity must be built on the same foundation. The one, single, sovereign subject of our lives should be, even at the price of martyrdom, conformity to God's will. We advance in vice rather than in virtue when we do, not God's will, but our own.

༺

Chapter Thirty-Three

Resign yourself to God's will
even amid suffering

Through freely consenting to become the Mother of
God, Mary experienced mentally all the bitterness of
Christ's Passion and death. Her mind's eye daily wit-
nessed the sufferings of her divine Son.

At the very beginning of His public ministry, "the
kings of the earth stood up, and the princes met together,
against the Lord and against His Christ."[167] Mary observed
their diabolical hatred, their hellish jealousy; she beheld
them spreading the false accusations that would compass
His Crucifixion. She was a martyr by anticipation, because she suffered in spirit the anguish and desolation
that afflicted her at the foot of the Cross. Each event
of the sorrowful drama was a sword that pierced her

[167] Ps. 2:2.

maternal heart. As any other mother might have done, Mary indulged the sad pleasure of examining each particular of the sufferings foretold for Christ, and faith increased her melancholy joy by enabling her to view His Passion in its true perspective: His vehement yearning to glorify His Father by His death, the greatest proof of His love for Him and for souls.

The Apostles, who had abandoned their Master, informed Mary of her Son's betrayal by Judas and of His brutal capture after His agony. The Beloved Disciple narrated to her what he had seen in the houses of Annas and Caiphas: how Christ had been branded as a blasphemer for His assertion that He was the Son of God. She saw Christ brought first to Pilate, then to Herod and again returned to the Roman governor. She beheld some of the outrages to which He was subjected before each ruler; the others were described to her. When she beheld the populace, rocked into anarchy by passion, unable to mask its hatred of Christ, and Pilate, the pitiful victim of his own vacillation, sitting in judgment, she concluded, with a woman's keenness of perception, that there was no hope for her divine Son. She suffered the humiliating embarrassment of seeing Barabbas preferred to Him when the

Roman governor showed the "Man of Sorrows"[168] to the wildly infuriated mob. And what a spectacle met her eyes as she gazed upon her Child with His flesh torn from His body, His head encircled with sharp thorns, His whole form robed in the ruby raiment of His blood — a mock King with a reed in His hand and a tattered cloak over His bleeding shoulders.

All this was for Mary but the prelude to greater sorrows. She heard the rabble, led by the chief priests, and intoxicated with the malice of Hell, clamoring for Christ's Crucifixion. She saw the gigantic Cross placed on His bent and mangled shoulders. Her heart sank lower within her each time He fell beneath its overpowering weight. Speechless with grief, she witnessed His virginal flesh torn from His bruised and battered body when the soldiers pitilessly tore off His garments. Transfixed with sorrow, she beheld His arms and feet roughly extended on the hard wood of the Cross. But what must have been her anguish when she saw the sacred body of her Child, every nerve vibrating with agonizing pain, twitch and convulse as the long, knife-edged nails were driven into

[168]Isa. 53:3.

its most delicately sensitive parts! She saw the Cross dragged to a hole into which the soldiers let it drop with a rough thud that violently shocked the entire body of the transpierced Redeemer. She heard the mob, not yet satisfied with their diabolical work, continue to torment their dying Victim.

Who can plumb the depths of Mary's grief or gauge her supernatural strength and her admirable resignation to God's will? Her agony beggars description. But she had still more to suffer in order to become the Queen of Martyrs.

Although worn and wasted with sorrow, she at once took her place at the foot of the Cross. There she stood with heavenly fortitude, her eyes fastened on her divine Son. How magnanimous was the sacrifice that she made of her dearest treasure as a holocaust to the inexorable justice of His outraged Father! How freely, how courageously she united the oblation of her own incomprehensible suffering and grief with the offering of Christ, thus proving herself worthy not only to share, but also to be one with Him, in the redemption of souls. Her own death would have been for her a far cheaper price for the salvation of sinners than the heart-sickening contemplation of the bitter Passion and death that Christ underwent to ransom them.

In that period of life through which every child of Adam seems to pass, whether in youth, in middle age, or in old age, when "grief . . . whispers the o'erfraught heart, and bids it break,"[169] let us stand with Mary at the foot of the Cross and learn from her resignation to the will of God. No other, after Christ, has taught us how to accept and bear suffering with the eloquence of Mary, the sorrowful Mother of God, the Queen of Martyrs.

---

[169]William Shakespeare, *Macbeth*, Act 4, scene 3.

Chapter Thirty-Four

⚭

Cherish Mary your mother

The parting with her dying divine Son was the apex of
Mary's anguish. Standing heroically at the foot of the
Cross, she paid the cost of becoming the Mother of
Christ by willingly consigning Him to a death whose
torture and shame depress the mind and sicken the heart.
For souls, she lovingly drained with Christ the chalice
of bitterest suffering, when, with utter self-extinction,
she exchanged the Son of God for the son of Zebedee.
"Woman," said the dying Redeemer, glancing at St. John,
"behold thy son."[170]

How the sorrow of separation must have wrung Mary's
maternal heart! But with the same humility with which
she had conceived Him, she consented to the supreme
loss of her God.

[170]John 19:26.

Christ's commendation of His mother to St. John is replete with spiritual significance.

The Savior had delivered Himself in His Passion to the will of His Father. "My Father," He had said, "if it be possible, let this chalice pass from me. Nevertheless, not as I wilt, but as Thou wilt."[171] And before His sacrifice for sinners could be perfect, He had to be forsaken by that Father. In the same way, Mary, who freely delivered her Son to the cruelest of deaths, extinguished, by parting with Christ, the light of her life for the perfection of her own self-annihilation. Only thus could she become one with her God in the salvation of souls. Both victims in the tragedy of Calvary had to be wholly immolated.

Why, it may be asked, did Mary undergo so willingly and so lovingly such overwhelming suffering? Why did she increase her sorrow when it was already as great as the sea? In submitting to pain and desolation indescribable, Mary wished, through correspondence with God's will, to perfect her virtue. She yearned to be Christ's most perfect imitator and, by so doing, to merit the title of Queen of Saints, an honor worthy only of the Mother of God.

[171]Matt. 26:39.

When God asks an extraordinary sacrifice of a soul, the object of His special love, He would have the soul die completely to itself, and so perfect its holocaust. Union with Jesus and Mary in their abandonment is the only refuge for such a soul.

In His commendation of Mary to the Beloved Disciple, Christ showed His loving solicitude for her material welfare by providing her, who was extremely poor, with a means of support. When He said to St. John, "Behold thy mother,"[172] He bade him to respect, revere, and love the Blessed Virgin as his mother. Such a bequeathal did not augur for Mary a life of ease and comfort. But it did serve partially to alleviate the bitterness of her sorrowful existence, deprived as she would be of her divine Son. The Apostle of Love obeyed the command of our Lord, because he took the Virgin to his own, provided for her, and loved her as his mother.

It is the teaching of the Fathers of the Church that St. John was our representative on Calvary and that Mary became, in his person, our mother. What gift could Christ give us, after the gift of Himself, more precious

[172] John 19:27.

than that! With her heart breaking with sorrow, Mary had to die a spiritual death in order to become our spiritual mother. No tongue can tell the magnitude and intensity of her love for souls washed by the blood of Christ, for which she endured pain and sorrow beyond conception. In becoming our mother, she became the Queen of Martyrs.

What a truly marvelous privilege is ours! Mary being our mother, we share in her love of her divine Son. Let us stand in spirit on the mount of crucifixion and listen to the dying Christ saying to each of us, "Behold thy mother." How stupendous is this gift! Christ gives us her whom He loved so much that He exhausted His power, so to speak, to exalt her — His dearest possession — above all other creatures. "Having loved His own who were in the world, He loved them unto the end."[173]

Yes, Christ exhausted His love for man. It was not enough for the infinite Lover of souls to free us from the slavery of Hell by His passion and death and to bestow upon us His body and blood, soul and divinity. He had to

[173]John 13:1.

crown the largess of His love with the munificent gift of His mother.

What is our appreciation of this priceless gift? We can best thank Christ for His extraordinary dying bequest by striving daily to emulate St. John in his love and veneration for Mary. But love and veneration for our Mother means only one thing: imitating her humility, her purity, her detachment from the world, and her unselfish resignation to the will of God in every event of her life. It also means unlimited confidence in her maternal intercession if we should ever have the misfortune of straying far from Christ by sin.

Mary cannot forsake us, because she is our Mother. If we confide our salvation to her loving care and faithfully imitate her virtues, she will fold us to her Immaculate Heart both now and at the hour of our death.

Chapter Thirty-Five

⚬

Realize how precious you are to Jesus and Mary

More courageous than the martyrs, Mary stood at the foot of the Cross and saw her divine Son bow His head and die. Her sorrow and distress of soul are incredible as she hears Him exclaim, "My God, my God, why hast Thou forsaken me?"[174] These words are but a poor expression of the desolation that wrung the soul of Christ with heart-breaking grief as His love for sinners soared to the summit of perfect self-extinction and reconciled the lost world with His eternal Father. Without divine comfort, His mind darkened with the spiritual gloom of our fallen nature, His heart laden with the concentrated iniquities of a doomed race, Christ, solitary and desolate, experienced the withering anguish of man's separation from His God by sin.

[174]Matt. 27:46.

If we understood the strength of Mary's love for her divine Son, we could comprehend the intensity of her sorrow as the woeful wail of the dying Christ fell on her ears. Indeed, the suffering of Christ in His dereliction was a mystery unintelligible even to His mother. And, without doubt, it was the hardest test of her faith. The mutual love of the Father and Son was coeval with Their very existence. Christ could not, then, have tried the faith of His mother more severely than by having her behold — at the very moment when, by His death for sinners, He was glorifying His heavenly Father most — His abandonment by that Father with whom He was eternally one.

But were it possible for Christ's cry of uttermost desolation to have weakened Mary's faith, His docile resignation to His eternal Father would have deepened it beyond comprehension. Amid the ghastly horror and chaos of the scene, how sweet to her ears were the consoling words of Christ's act of perfect obedience to the will of His Father: "Father, into Thy hands I commend my spirit."[175] In union with her divine Son, she, too, does

[175]Luke 23:46.

the will of God perfectly. Oh, how strong was her faith when her soul was most seared with searching sorrow!

If God, in His love for us — "for whom the Lord loveth, He chastiseth"[176] — should send us a cross in the shape of harrowing mental pain, and we feel the heart-sickening sense of desolation, let us turn to Jesus and Mary for supernatural strength in order that we, like them, may abandon ourselves to the divine will. Then will we die wholly to ourselves and be able to say with the dying Christ, "It is consummated."[177]

When Mary heard her divine Son utter these words and saw Him bow His head and die, she died a spiritual death whose suffering defies description. So poignant was the pain of her gentle, sinless soul that, when the darkness of night swallowed up the light of day, for the reason that nature was mourning her God, when the rocks were rent asunder, when the earth was in the throes of terrorizing convulsions, even when the dead appeared, she heard and saw nothing. Her only concern was her dead Child.

[176]Heb. 12:6.
[177]John 19:30.

Gazing sorrowfully on His lifeless body, she watched Longinus drive the spear into His heart.[178] The words of Simeon were then verified: "And thy own soul a sword shall pierce."[179]

She stood motionless, observing every detail of the gruesome tragedy that had robbed her of Him whom she loved more than her life. Mute with grief, she witnessed His disciples remove the nails from the Redeemer's hands and feet, extract the thorns from His head, and take Him down from the Cross. What a sight met her tear-dimmed eyes when she beheld the body of her Son at close range, with its gaping wounds, crimsoned with blood, bruised and mangled, every bone numbered, the victim of inhuman barbarity inspired by the hatred of Hell! Her soul so filled with overpowering love and sorrow that death would have been a relief, she embraced the once ravishingly beautiful countenance of her Child, now haggard with the pallor of death. She accompanied His mortal remains to the tomb and then, leaning on the arm of St. John, retired heart-broken.

[178] John 19:34.
[179] Luke 2:35.

Who could see, from tears refraining,
Christ's dear Mother uncomplaining
In so great a sorrow bowed?

Who, unmoved, behold her languish
Underneath His Cross of anguish,
'Mid the fierce, unpitying crowd!

For His people's sins th' all-Holy
She beheld a Victim lowly,
Bleed in torments, bleed and die.

Saw her Well-beloved taken,
Saw her Child in death forsaken,
Heard His last expiring cry.

What a world of sorrow, what an inexhaustible theme, is this saddest drama ever enacted on earth! The eternal God, Christ our Lord, crucified as a public malefactor between two thieves! Mary, His mother, spiritually crucified, her sorrow great as her love!

Oh, how precious are our souls to Jesus and Mary, our blood Brother and our mother. The best expression of our gratitude for such love is the irrevocable consecration of ourselves to them — in the gloom of uncertainty, in the anguish of doubt, in the heart-riving loneliness of interior desolation, when God seems to desert us, by complete abandonment to the divine will.

Chapter Thirty-Six

Strive to die to yourself

From a natural standpoint, the life of Christ was a categoric contradiction of the glorious prophecy of the archangel Gabriel. Judged by worldly standards, it was a monumental failure. But what a success, eternal in its import, was Christ's earthly career in the light of the marvelous miracle of His Resurrection! How fully does He realize by this amazing mystery every promise made by the angelic messenger to Mary when he announced to her that she was to be the Mother of God!

The embassy of Gabriel must therefore be understood only in a spiritual sense, because Christ's kingdom was to be not of this world. His Resurrection was to be the beginning of that kingdom which was to last forever: "Of His kingdom there shall be no end."[180]

[180]Luke 1:33.

Christ had repeatedly told His Apostles that He would rise on the third day after His death. It is unthinkable that He would withhold this information from His mother, whose suffering was, in proportion to the pre-eminently superior supernatural texture of her faith, far greater than theirs. Nothing could shake Mary's belief that her Son would rise again. But her faith was purely spiritual. It proved no antidote to the bitter suffering that she endured throughout her life, and especially during the Passion and death of her divine Son.

There are times when Christ seems to crush souls most dear to Him. But without diminishing the rigor of their suffering, He at the same time gives them a glimpse of the reward for their faithful endeavor to bear the Cross as He did. Like Mary, they understand that "the sufferings of this time are not worthy to be compared with the glory to come."[181] But such knowledge gives them no comfort during the time of trial. Hence, like her, they experience the full weight of the Cross.

After His Resurrection, Christ certainly did not wish to deprive His mother of this overwhelming proof of His

[181]Rom. 8:18.

divinity by failing to appear to her. Why, then, do the evangelists mention not even one apparition of the Savior to Mary? Do they seek to convey thus that the Blessed Mother was a mere automaton in the gigantic work of man's redemption? Does their silence indicate that Christ thought more of His Apostles than of His own mother? By no means!

The evangelists disclose the apparitions of the Redeemer to His Apostles because the Apostles were called by Christ to bear witness to the truth of His teaching by proclaiming to the utmost bounds of the earth the irrefragable proof of their Master's divinity. Such, however, was not the vocation of Mary. But even to doubt that Christ appeared to the Blessed Virgin — and many times — would be equivalent to a denial of His love for her. It was Mary's self-effacement, her unparalleled humility, that caused her to conceal the truth of these visitations, which were divinely consoling and comforting to her.

Since she was the most perfect follower of her divine Son, her love of suffering was so unselfish that she never desired these apparitions. Although to see her Son glorious and immortal gave joy indescribable to her soul, she would have been content, had such been the will of God, to learn from the Apostles that Christ had risen from the dead. Like Christ, Mary never sought her own glory. Our Lord rose from the dead, not to please Himself, but to glorify His Father. In imitation of her divine Son, Mary's detachment, which is the essence of virtue, was without any thought of self-gratification. The glory of God was the end and aim of her lifelong practice of heroic holiness.

When God demands of a soul a great sacrifice, He strengthens the soul, through the vivifying power of His grace, to overcome all obstacles. Such a soul dies perfectly to itself, and its only desire is to remain spiritually dead to its natural inclinations as long as God wishes. This spiritual self-extinction is a perplexing mystery to the selfish soul. Why, it asks, should a soul yearn to remain spiritually dead with Christ? The soul enamored of itself fails to realize the meaning of the words "Christ died for all, that they also who live may not now live to themselves, but unto Him who died for them and rose again."[182]

[182] 2 Cor. 5:15.

Fidelity to grace made both Mary's spiritual death and her spiritual resurrection perfect. She anticipated neither the one nor the other, but patiently awaited God's time for the action of His grace. When He so determined, she died to herself and rose to the highest degree of sanctity.

Such must be our dispositions if we would imitate Mary perfectly. Like her, we must die absolutely to ourselves; otherwise we cannot rise with her and thus lead eminently virtuous lives. Total death to our natural selves is the price of our spiritual resurrection.

Chapter Thirty-Seven

Be willing to sacrifice all for God

Holy Scripture does not state that Mary was present at
Christ's Ascension. But who would be so skeptical as to
doubt that Christ bade farewell to His mother and that
she was present in honor when He ate for the last time
with His Apostles?

She saw His sacred body, immortal and impassible,
raised on high and dazzling His disciples with its resplen-
dent glory. Their look of intense concentration betrayed
the yearning of their hearts to ascend to Heaven with
Him, their Lord and Master. As we have but the crudest
notion of Mary's love for Christ, we have the most superficial idea of the vehemence of her longing for eternal
union with Him. With a supernatural ardor too deep for
expression, she ascended with Him spiritually.

Christ's ascension perfected Mary's understanding of
the eternal meaning of suffering. That she associated the

idea of suffering with its everlasting reward as she gazed with burning love at her divine Son returning triumphantly to His eternal Father requires no flight of the imagination to believe. In beholding Christ, the King of Martyrs, ascending to Heaven to take possession of His glory, she realized that, as Queen of Martyrs, as Christ's most perfect follower, she would one day share in His eternal recompense.

After the Ascension of her divine Son, the pleasures and pursuits of this life had for Mary no attraction. Her heart was in Heaven with her Child and her God. As she had lost Him whose presence ravished her soul, she doubtless repeated endlessly with the royal psalmist, "What have I in Heaven? And besides Thee, what do I desire upon earth? For Thee my flesh and my heart hath fainted away. Thou art the God of my heart and the God that is my portion forever."[183] The eagerness of her longing for eternal union with Christ contended with her yearning to do His will, which had spiritually crucified her by demanding that she remain on earth, deprived in her exile of Him, her treasure. But such was Mary's love of the

[183]Ps. 72:25-26 (RSV = Ps. 73:25-26).

divine will that she joyously sacrificed her own happiness and gladly relinquished her God, whom she loved beyond understanding. She who had heroically delivered Him to the most terrible of deaths also immolated Him in Heaven by dying to the desire to be united with Him. Her self-extinction was perfect.

To comprehend the suffering of Mary during this protracted period, we would have to be bound to Christ as closely as she was, both naturally and supernaturally. What a mighty conflict raged within her! Her love of Christ, which wafted her in spirit to His side in Heaven, ever contended with her yearning to do His will by remaining on earth, deprived of His visible presence.

We would have to be as holy as Mary to experience such suffering.

What pain can equal the soul's supernaturally ardent, overmastering, but nevertheless unavailing desire to possess its God forever!

We are too carnal, our spirituality is too coarse, to undergo Mary's agonizing sense of loss. And yet, if we are to become saints, we must be prepared to accept and to use such a cross as the infallible means of advancing to the highest sanctity. Indeed, unless we do this, we do not keep perfectly the first and greatest commandment of the law. The love of God above all things implies loving submission to His providential dispensations, with no thought of the sacrifice He asks as the price of such submission. We have been made for God, and He alone can satisfy the highest and holiest aspirations of our hearts.

Oh, if the love of God burned within us, how unsatisfactory, how insipid, and how nauseating would everything else be to us! It is strange that we do not love with all our hearts, with all our minds, and with all our strength the God who loved us so much that He died the most heart-rending death for us.

But we cannot love God and ourselves simultaneously. Nor can the love of God and the love of the world coexist in our souls. The whole scheme of the Christian dispensation aims at only one thing: to kindle in our hearts the fire of divine love which Christ came to cast on earth. If our prayers and our seemingly fervent receptions of the sacraments of Penance and the Holy Eucharist fail to do this, they are practically worthless. Union with God through love is the supreme end of our creation. "The earth and the fullness thereof"[184] can therefore never satisfy the human heart. In this respect, experience does not seem to be the best teacher, because myriads try to appease their hunger for happiness with the love of the transitory.

The true child of Mary must be prepared to make the sacrifice necessary to overcome the love of created things with the love of the Creator.

[184]Ps. 23:1 (RSV = Ps. 24:1).

Chapter Thirty-Eight

∽

Let the Holy Spirit pray within you

Our Lord had foretold to His Apostles that the Holy Spirit, whom He promised to send them, would strengthen them with His grace and illumine their minds with His light to enable them better to grasp all the truths that He, their Savior, had already taught them as He walked with them as their elder Brother.

"These things have I spoken to you, abiding with you. But the Paraclete, the Holy Spirit, whom the Father will send in my name, He will teach you all things and bring all things to your mind, whatsoever I shall have said to you."[185]

With Mary, the Apostles prepared for the promised "Gift of God Most High." Prayer was the soul of their preparation. "All these were persevering with one mind

[185]John 14:25-26.

in prayer, with the women, and Mary, the mother of Jesus, and with His brethren."[186] For nine days, they refrained from all contact with the external world. During this precious time, they eschewed servile work. In silence and recollection, they occupied themselves with God alone. Great was the efficacy of their prayer, because they were praying with Mary. When we pray with Mary, God will always answer us.

As Mary surpassed the Apostles in virtue, their preparation for the reception of the Holy Spirit could not be compared with hers. She was to receive the largest and the richest outpouring of Christ's Spirit. She did not, therefore, pray alone. The Holy Spirit prayed within her. Thoroughly realizing that she was only a helpless, dependent creature, and so unable to prepare her soul to be a fit dwelling for the Holy Spirit, she besought His divine assistance with unwearying fervor. United with Him, her prayer breathed "the peace of God, which surpasseth all understanding"[187] and the love of God that was her paradise on earth.

[186] Acts 1:14.
[187] Phil. 4:7.

∞

When we depend on our own efforts in prayer, God will not hear us, because He "resisteth the proud."[188] In communing with God, we must surrender ourselves to the Holy Spirit, the Spirit of prayer.

Mary was the Queen of Saints; her life illustrated every phase of sanctity; her soul was a house of perfect prayer. Holiness so notable was, however, not the result of her own unaided exertions. It was due to the Holy Spirit, to whose guidance she abandoned herself. Her prayer was distinguished by the conscious knowledge of her own nothingness and the realization of the greatness of God. She prayed under the divine influence of the Holy Spirit and in the closest possible union with Him.

How signally different is our prayer! We pray as if the success of our prayer depended entirely on our own efforts. Every faculty is roused to action. Instead of controlling our imaginations, we allow them to wander capriciously. We believe that prayer, in order to be efficacious, must be voluble; we falsely persuade ourselves that

[188]James 4:6.

the crowning glory of prayer and the infallible test of its worth with God is the amount of energy that we put into it.

In her retreat with the Apostles, which was dedicated to unceasing prayer, Mary was the personification of religious calmness and composure. Her prayer came spontaneously and without mental agitation from her heart, enamored of God alone. One not thoroughly versed in this sacred science would conclude, from her unearthly tranquillity, that she was not praying at all.

When we examine too closely the workings of the powers of our souls, when we are anxious to know that our intellects, our wills, and our imaginations are functioning to the best of their ability, we are not, as we should be at the time of prayer, thinking of God, but of ourselves. Before we begin to pray, let us realize, following the example of Mary, that our own exertions when we address ourselves to God count for nothing. It is the Holy Spirit who must pray within us. Without His help, we cannot pray. "No man can say 'the Lord Jesus' but by the Holy Spirit."[189]

[189] 1 Cor. 12:3.

Realizing this truth, we will prepare for the reception of the Holy Spirit by effacing ourselves and, with deliberate calmness, bring every power of our souls under His divine influence. We will beg Him whom Christ promised as the source of all spiritual knowledge and discernment to create in us the dispositions that will delight Him to come and abide with us.

When we rely on our own efforts in prayer, when we resort to artificial stimulation by trying to assimilate the thought of others — in a word, when we perform this religious duty without the direction of the Holy Spirit — we can hardly expect Him to give us the graces that will make us true followers of Christ. Our prayer, like Mary's and the Apostles', must come from our hearts under the absolute dominion of the Holy Spirit.

The love of God above all things, detachment from the world, and an abiding sense of the supernatural, or recollection — these are the prerequisites of such prayer. After all, since we do not have a lasting city here, but seek one that is to come,[190] we should live as strangers and pilgrims ever sighing for our eternal home, by

[190]Cf. Heb. 13:14.

disengagement from creatures and by the habitual thought of God and what leads to Him. If we pray like our heavenly Mother, the Holy Spirit will greatly facilitate our salvation by bestowing on us His greatest graces.

Chapter Thirty-Nine

Strive to advance in perfection

That Mary could receive an increase of grace, after having been declared by the archangel to be full of grace, involves our minds in a web, so to speak, of mystification. But the human mind should not arrogate the power to unravel the mystery of God's infinite action on souls. According to earthly standards, nothing could be added to Mary's fullness of grace. According to God's eternal standards, the sanctity proclaimed by Gabriel was only the beginning of her unimaginable growth in holiness.

When Christ was conceived in her womb by the omnipotent power of the Holy Spirit, Mary possessed the Author of grace, and He so adorned her soul with the richness of His heavenly gift that she excited the wonder and incredulity of both men and angels. After the birth of her divine Son, the pearl of great price[191] gleamed more and more lustrous within her as it daily united her more closely with her God. The prime purpose of Mary's earthly martyrdom was to deepen and expand her sanctity. How many and how great, then, were the graces she received in order to attain to the eminent virtue that was hers when, on Calvary, she became the Queen of Martyrs.

As we cannot grasp the sublimity of Mary's sanctity, we cannot understand the measure of her grace. The gift that God conferred on the humble Virgin when He chose her to be the mother of His divine Son, and the grace commensurate with that gift, are incomprehensible. All that God could give He bestowed on Mary. The Holy Spirit overshadowed her at the Annunciation, and on Pentecost, He made her heart a furnace of divine love.

He did not enrich her, as He did the Apostles, with the wondrous gifts of miracles, tongues, and prophecy. But the gift He gave her was superior to them all: divine love. By her love of God above all things and of His adopted sons for His sake, she was to tower above all the

[191]Cf. Matt. 13:46.

Apostles combined in the spread of Christ's kingdom on earth.

Mary's labors in the extension of the Church were not, like those of each Apostle, confined to a special field, but were to embrace the whole world. Her work was to be effected, not by unmatched eloquence, not by the working of miracles, but by the ardor of her maternal love, which would make her a living holocaust for the souls of her children.

To accompany the Apostles while they fulfilled the duties of their ministry would ill accord with Mary's humility. In silence and solitude, by the efficacy of her prayers and the fervor of her charity, she was to be the master worker of them all. So great indeed was her love of humility that she did not even wish to see the tangible results of her truly miraculous power with her divine Son in the spread of the Faith that it cost both Him and her so much to give to mankind.

Not as fully in the hearts of the Apostles as in the heart of Mary did the Holy Spirit kindle the fire of His infinite love. Possessing, because of her plenitude of grace, an extraordinary capacity for divine love, she attracted the Spirit of love immeasurably more than all the Apostles collectively — attracted Him, as it were, irresistibly. She was now united with God more intimately than ever.

On Pentecost, a transformation was wrought in the soul of Mary more wondrous than the change worked in the souls of the Apostles. Their worldly views about the kingdom of God on earth were banished by the Spirit of God; under the influence of the Spirit, holiness of the highest order replaced their imperfections, and the cowardice of their self-preservation was conquered by a loving readiness to die for the spread of the Faith and the glory of God. But no taint of the slightest sin or the least shadow of imperfection had to be removed from Mary's virginal soul.

On the contrary, when she received the "Gift of God Most High," she stood on the mount of sanctity. Were we to deny or even to question this truth, we would limit God's power. We cannot constrain God's munificence to His creatures. Man is finite in his ability to receive God's gifts, but God's generosity to man cannot be diminished, because it is essentially infinite. Since, as creatures, we are capable of continual growth in virtue, we can easily understand that Mary progressed in sanctity to a degree baffling to the intelligence of the very angels.

∽

As our chief duty in life is the sanctification of our souls, we should strive with all our powers to advance to that standard of perfection that God has determined for each one of us. We should use all our efforts to grow daily in divine love.

This we can do by bearing in mind our total dependence upon God and hence our urgent need of ever corresponding with His grace. We will then accomplish God's will with a spiritual resiliency that will make the bitterest suffering most sweet to us.

We should try unceasingly to understand something of Mary's love of humility, and God's love of her in keeping her soul divinely beautiful with this exquisite virtue. Without humility we will not advance, no matter how hard we may try, in the way of God.

∞

Chapter Forty

Adorn your soul with Mary's virtues

Even if we were gifted with the intelligence of an angel, we would not be able to understand fully Mary's love for her divine Son. Therefore we have no way of determining the intensity of her longing, after His Ascension, to be united with Him forever. Mary's love for Christ was as much deeper and more expansive than the total love of all the saints for Him as the depth and breadth of the sea compared with the rivulets that flow into it. Her suffering was at the same time the purest act of love.

The preamble to pain so pleasing is abandonment to God and a willingness to submit to the greatest loss and subsequent desolation of soul. Only when we lose all do we find all. The love of God will be perfected in us and will purify our thoughts and desires only when we die to ourselves. Divine love daily strove to disengage Mary's soul from her body. Gradually undermined by its unceasing activity, her enfeebled energies were forced to surrender to its violence. Finally breaking its fetters, her soul flew to the eternal embrace of her infinite Lover. Like Christ, Mary died of love.

As the body of her divine Son was preserved from the corruption of the grave, so, too, she from whom He took flesh was, unlike any other creature, free from the dominion of earthly decay. How could Mary's body, which was the living tabernacle of the eternal God, the temple of the Holy Trinity, crumble into dust? Dissolution is not only a law of nature (for nothing earthly lasts) but also a sequel of sin. Mary was sinless. She was thus exempt from the universal law. Her virginal flesh could not suffer contamination.

It has been the belief of the Church in all ages that Mary's body was assumed into Heaven shortly after her death. The Church has put her official seal on her belief by establishing the feast of the Assumption.

Mary is now enthroned in Heaven, body and soul, by the side of her divine Son. The Savior has made the Assumption of His mother a fitting climax to His own Incarnation. There is an essential correlation among the mysteries of Christianity. "If Mary at one time received Christ our Savior on earth, it was proper that the Savior, in turn, should receive Mary in Heaven. Having deigned to come down to her, He should raise her up to Himself in order that she should enter into glory," says Bossuet.[192]

"Oh, how does the source of life," remarks St. John Damascene, "pass through death to life? Oh, how can she obey the law of nature who, in conceiving, surpasses the boundaries of nature? How is her spotless body made subject to death? In order to be clothed with immortality, she must first put off mortality, since the God of nature did not reject the penalty of death. She dies according to the flesh, destroys death by death, and through corruption gains incorruption, and makes her death the source of resurrection."

What a scene of heavenly beauty, grandeur, and magnificence was Mary's Assumption! Before this gorgeous pageant, transcending the highest flight of fancy, human eloquence pales. Her body borne by the angels and shining more brilliantly than the sun, all her powers transfigured to an inconceivable degree, she is greeted by her divine Son in words that the Sacred Scriptures may

[192]Jacques Bénigne Bossuet (1627-1704), French preacher and Bishop of Meaux.

perhaps be permitted to suggest to us: "Winter is now past; the rain is over and gone. The flowers have appeared in our land. . . . The fig tree hath put forth her green figs; the vines in the flower yield their sweet smell. Arise, my love, my beautiful one, and come. Come from Libanus, my spouse, come from Libanus, come; thou shalt be crowned."[193]

Surely the heavenly hosts that at Christ's birth had chanted the sublime symphony of reconciliation, ravished by her beauty, must repeat with ever-increasing rapture the glorious refrain: "Who is this that cometh up from the desert, flowing with delights, leaning upon her Beloved? . . . Who is she that cometh forth as the morning rising, fair as the moon, bright as the sun, terrible as an army set in array?"[194] It is Mary, the Mother of Christ and our mother!

Exalted above the nine choirs of the angels and above all the saints, and before the assembled heavenly court, Mary is crowned their queen by the eternal God and thus wields unlimited power with Him. This superb scene,

[193]Cant. 2:11-13, 4:8 (RSV = Song of Sol. 2:11-13, 4:8).
[194]Cant. 8:5, 6:9 (RSV = Song of Sol. 8:5, 6:9).

inferior in stately magnificence only to Christ's Ascension, wafts us above the bourne of time into the realms of the blessed.

Not because of the superabundant gifts of God, but because she was faithful to His grace — this was the reason for Mary's munificent reward. And to imitate her in this is the one duty imperative on all of us. While we shall never be as holy as our heavenly Mother, since the measure of our grace will always be inferior to hers, we must adorn our souls with virtue through correspondence with the degree of grace that God bestows on us. Thus will we walk in her footsteps and, like her, grow in humility, in purity, and in love of God.

O Mary, our Mother, with thine arms outstretched —
those tender arms in which the eternal God
delighted to dwell when He became our blood Brother —
plead our cause. With thine eyes of mercy,
beseech of Him for us, thy children,
the grace that in our exile we may resemble thee,
His most devoted follower, and so at last,
in union with thee, may glorify Him forever!

John A. Kane
(1883-1962)

Born in Philadelphia in 1883, John Kane attended St. Mary's Seminary in Baltimore, Maryland, and St. Charles Borromeo Seminary in Overbrook, Pennsylvania, and was ordained for the Archdiocese of Philadelphia in 1912.

Known for his devotion to the Holy Eucharist, Fr. Kane was the first pastor in his archdiocese to introduce and to receive permission to hold all-night adoration of the Blessed Sacrament. He placed great importance on Catholic education of the young and succeeded in filling to overflowing his parish school of St. Madeline's in Ridley Park. In addition, he actively sought to educate adults in their Faith, and he was a pioneer in initiating a weekly religious class for them.

Fr. Kane was known during his lifetime for his great love of prayer and meditation, and his several books give

The School of Mary

proof of the wisdom gleaned from so many hours of
contemplation. His writings bespeak a profound love
of Christ and a warm understanding of the Catholic lay-
man's struggle to achieve holiness. His words offer Catholics practical insight and encouragement to seek a
deeper union and friendship with God.

❧

Sophia Institute Press®

Sophia Institute is a nonprofit institution that seeks to restore man's knowledge of eternal truth, including man's knowledge of his own nature, his relation to other persons, and his relation to God. Sophia Institute Press® serves this end in numerous ways: it publishes translations of foreign works to make them accessible for the first time to English-speaking readers; it brings out-of-print books back into print; and it publishes important new books that fulfill the ideals of Sophia Institute. These books afford readers a rich source of the enduring wisdom of mankind.

Sophia Institute Press® makes these high-quality books available to the general public by using advanced technology and by soliciting donations to subsidize its general publishing costs. Your generosity can help Sophia Institute Press® to provide the public with editions of works containing the enduring wisdom of the ages. Please send your tax-deductible contribution to the address below. We also welcome your questions, comments, and suggestions.

For your free catalog, call:

Toll-free: 1-800-888-9344

or write:

Sophia Institute Press®

Box 5284

Manchester, NH 03108

or visit our website:

www.sophiainstitute.com